MY 30 DAYS
UNDER THE OVERPASS

[NOT YOUR ORDINARY DEVOTIONAL]

BY MIKE YANKOSKI

MULTNOMAH
BOOKS

MY 30 DAYS UNDER THE OVERPASS
© 2006 by Michael G. Yankoski III

International Standard Book Number: 978-1-59052-668-2

Interior design and typeset by Katherine Lloyd, The DESK

Scripture quotations are from:
The Holy Bible, *English Standard Version* (ESV)
© 2001 by Crossway Bibles, a division of Good News Publishers.
Used by permission. All rights reserved.

Published in the United States by WaterBrook Multnomah, an imprint of the
Crown Publishing Group, a division of Penguin Random House LLC,
New York.

MULTNOMAH and its mountain colophon are registered trademarks
of Penguin Random House LLC.

Printed in the United States of America

For information:
MULTNOMAH BOOKS
12265 ORACLE BOULEVARD, SUITE 200
COLORADO SPRING, CO 80921

Library of Congress Cataloging-in-Publication Data
Yankoski, Michael.
    My 30 days under the overpass : (not your ordinary devotional) / by Mike Yankoski.
        p. cm.
    Includes bibliographical references.
    ISBN 1-59052-668-6
  1. Church work with the homeless--Prayer-books and devotions--English. 2.
Yankoski, Michael.
I. Title. II. Title: My thirty days under the overpass.
    BV4456.Y36 2006
    261.8'325--dc22

                          2006008684

15—10 9 8 7 6

TABLE OF CONTENTS

WEEK THREE

WEEK FOUR

FOREWORD

very Christian must answer this question: What does my faith mean when I'm away from church and Christian friends, when I'm outside of my comfort zone, and when "things aren't going my way"? The reality is if we don't have faith in these times, if we only "talk the talk," then we miss the point. If we are truly Christian, truly "Christ-like," then we have to be walking where Christ walked—among the poor, the "sinners," and the challenging aspects of life. It is here that our faith is real.

Mike Yankoski practices hard Christianity, first in action, then in words. He hangs out with alcoholics, drug addicts, and mental cases. He beds down in rescue missions and under bridges. He panhandles for bus fare and eats what he can scrounge from dumpsters and throwaway food. Yes, he has guts. But he also has faith. Mike takes Christ at His word and challenges readers to summon the courage to live the real Christian faith.

Be careful before you go further in this devotional. Mike says it himself: "Put this book down if you're not willing to put your lifestyle where your mouth is." It might make you uncomfortable, or make you ask hard questions of yourself. But we need to be asking these hard questions if we are going to follow Jesus. Not all of us are called to live on the street for five months, but we are called to the kind of real, sacrificial love for others that Mike demonstrates. Jesus is alive under the overpass, and by loving others there, we demonstrate our love for Him.

—Dean R. Hirsch
President, World Vision International

ON-RAMP

This is not your average devotional—you know, pure sweetness and inspiration...the kind that gives you that little emotional *whoosh*, that reminds you that, sure enough, you *do* believe all the right things!

Actually, this book isn't really about belief, at least not in the traditional sense. In fact, you should put this book down if you're not willing to put your lifestyle where your mouth is. It will be a waste of your time. And frankly, it will be confusing to others who have the idea that you're going to live a certain way and then you don't. You might as well watch exercise videos while you sit on your couch eating bonbons and potato chips. Same idea.

My 30 Days Under the Overpass isn't a book you just read. You *do* it too.

The idea to become homeless for five months came when I realized I was saying a lot of stuff, but not doing anything. Don't worry, I'm not suggesting you go out and become homeless. But I am asking you to engage, find a place where your beliefs can become actions.

Maybe you've had a chance to read *Under the Overpass*, the book that details my journey on the streets of America with my traveling partner, Sam. Maybe not. Either way, it's fine. *My 30 Days Under the Overpass* actually goes a little deeper into the heart of some of the issues we encountered during our time on the streets. If you'd like a detailed description of the whole journey from start to finish, check out *Under the Overpass*. I'll just give you the short version here.

The idea to become homeless hit me quite suddenly one morning during my freshman year of college. I was sitting in church, not really paying much attention to the sermon, when suddenly—for no reason that I could figure—I jolted awake and began listening. The pastor was pushing us to be the Christians we say we are. By the end of the message I was convinced of something I didn't like—I wasn't living up to my words at all.

I was being a complete hypocrite.

Ouch.

I had a comfortable life as a student at a Christian college in Santa Barbara. Where was my self-sacrifice? Where was the love of others? Where was the willingness to let God lead me where He wanted? My Christianity, my faith, was a strong set of beliefs, but not much more. Rarely did it engage the real world, and when it did, it usually did so only with an under-the-breath prayer for some heathen who had just cut me off on the freeway.

The more I thought about it, the more I had a sinking feeling that I was making a mockery of what I said was the most important thing in the world. I was actually, as the apostle Paul says, crucifying Christ again because I was only pretending this stuff was real, and only when it was convenient for me (see Hebrews 6:4–6).

Then, out of nowhere came the idea to live on the streets. It was really just a mental picture of me sitting under a bridge, long hair, unkempt appearance, panhandling in order to survive. At that moment, I wondered what it would be like if I *was* the homeless man in my head and I happened to encounter the falsely pious me, the guy who had only recently awoken from his mid-sermon slumber. If I was hungry and met someone like me, would my need be met? Or would the person simply walk away and leave me, stomach growling, frustrated and jaded by the people who merely *said* they believed in unconditional love?

Tough questions. Questions I couldn't shake.

Actually deciding to *become* homeless didn't happen

quickly. Rather, it was the result of more than a year and a half of thought, research, planning, prayer, and preparation. Over the course of the next sixteen months, between January of my freshman year and May of my sophomore year, I poured over other people's research, volunteered at the local rescue mission, and did everything I knew to do to get ready for the journey I felt compelled to take.

In the spring of my sophomore year, I awoke late one evening, absolutely horrified by the realization that this crazy journey was actually going to happen, but that I had been proceeding on my own, without seeking wise counsel as the Bible instructs (see Proverbs 19:20).

The next day I began forming an official board of advisers, asking professors, pastors, rescue-mission presidents, and other men close to me to form a group and act as advisers in preparation for this journey. Surprisingly, they all agreed, and my council was formed. These men proved to be instrumental in helping me set my goals and plan out the details of the journey.

But as the departure date drew nearer, one big puzzle piece was still missing: someone to journey with. (Only a fool journeys alone. Frodo had Sam Gamgee, right?) Most of the guys I'd asked to join me couldn't quite catch the vision. Imagine that! *Hey, anybody want to go hang out under a bridge in the rain with me?* Others who were interested had been advised against the idea by their counsel. I had actually surrendered to the idea of going alone when I met Sam.

Sam happened to be in Santa Barbara visiting his older brother. One afternoon he came to see friends on my campus, where I ran into him. After a short game of Frisbee, Sam and I started talking about my crazy idea. Miraculously, Sam was interested. We agreed to each pray about traveling together, seek counsel, and then talk again in two weeks.

I'll never forget the excitement in Sam's voice when he called. "Let's do this!" he said as soon I answered. I had my traveling partner.

The end of my sophomore year came all too quickly. The last few days between taking my final exams and packing for the drive home, I was furiously e-mailing my advisers, making last-minute preparations, and finalizing plans.

I had to be moved out of my dorm room by 5 p.m. on a Friday. It's a seventeen-hour drive from my college to my home in Colorado. I prefer to push through the drive in one shift. Of course, caffeine is essential. But by the time

I was finished packing, I had been awake for nearly twenty-six hours and could hardly see straight. Exhausted and without a room to sleep in, I decided to sleep outside on campus. Why not? In just a few weeks this would be normal. I decided to roll out my sleeping bag near the gymnasium.

At about 11 p.m., merely one hour before I was to get up and begin the long drive home, I awoke with a start, sensing something in the bushes near my head. Without my contacts in or glasses on, I flipped over onto my stomach and noticed a small ball of fur only a foot away from my face.

A second later, I was slammed in the face with the most toxic, putrid, and painful liquid I've ever known. I leaped up, coughing, sputtering, sneezing, and blinded by the tears now pouring from my eyes. Then my sleeping bag got tangled around my feet, sending me spinning backward to the ground.

Yes, it's true. I was sprayed in the face by a skunk from less than a foot away. And I hadn't even begun my journey yet. (God sometimes has interesting ways to prepare us for what He has in store for us.)

For the next week, I shampooed with tomato sauce every chance I got (which doesn't really work, by the way).

By then, Sam and I were both in Colorado and ready to depart for the streets.

We were setting off on a journey that would take us to six cities: Denver; Washington DC; Portland; San Francisco; Phoenix; and San Diego. Our purposes were clear and well-defined:

To better understand the life of the homeless in America and to see firsthand how the church is responding to their needs.

To encourage others to "live out loud" for Christ in whatever ways God is asking them to.

To learn personally what it means to depend on Christ for our daily physical needs, and to experience contentment and confidence in Him.

On May 27, 2003, Sam and I stepped off—or rather, leaped off—the solid ground of our comfort, trusting the Lord to catch us and teach us and use us in whatever ways He saw fit. What followed were five months of difficult nights spent under bridges, embarrassing episodes digging through trash cans, painful rejections, incredible conversations with the homeless, and a different perspective on the church. Having felt rejection from many Christians, those homeless months continue to push me today to align my life with the Bible through real examples of love.

It's so easy for God's love to make a real difference in someone else's life if we're willing to step outside of what's comfortable.

That's what this book is about. It's designed to take you deeper into some scriptural examples of how to treat others, maybe even people who are really different than you are, and hopefully help you live a life worthy of the gospel of Christ (see Philippians 1:27). Sunday through Friday we'll look at different passages of Scripture, different quotes from past Christian writers, and stories from Sam's and my time on the streets. Every day has a principle that I will ask you to apply directly and prayerfully to your life, and to the people you interact with every day. Then comes Saturday—the Action Day. Each Saturday I recommend three different activities to help get you in the mindset of service. Humility and a serving attitude are not things that come easily for many of us. Service takes practice. So on these days we're going to *do* things that make the scriptural principles tangible.

This book is about pushing you to change the way you live and the way you think about yourself, your world, and your God—and it's about how all these things interact in your life, how what you believe cannot really ever be separate from what you do.

Thanks for coming along on our journey, one day at a time, by reading this book. My hope and prayer is that God would use it to help encourage you to continue in your journey with Him, and when it's necessary, leap off of your comfortable, solid world into His eternal arms.

Here we go.

(Watch out for skunks.)

GUT CHECK 1.0

Flip on tonight's news or go to a news blog and you'll learn all about the wretched things that are going on in our world—famines, epidemics, earthquakes, hurricanes, rapes, beatings, political chaos, slavery, human trafficking, just to name a few. When you look at all of it, it's enough to make you feel really, really small, like there's no way you can make an impact.

Well, I want to let you in on a little secret: The world is not yours to change. *None* of us is big enough, influential enough, or powerful enough to end any one of the world's major issues. The only person powerful enough to eradicate poverty or cure all disease or stop earthquakes is Jesus. But He didn't do any of that. Jesus, in His wisdom, knew He couldn't just come down here and fix everything for us; He knew we wouldn't learn anything that way. Instead, He showed us how to live by spending thirty years on earth, setting the ultimate example for us to follow. He didn't end poverty. Instead, He reminded us that "you always have the poor with you" (see Mark 14:7).

But that doesn't mean Jesus did nothing to help the poor, nothing to reach out to those whom everyone else shunned. Instead, He lived with them, listened to them, ate with them (sometimes He brought the food), partied with them, healed them, wept and laughed with them...

Same with us. Yes, the world is messed up. There are a lot of hurting people and a lot of important issues. You can't end poverty, stop earthquakes, or feed every person on the planet. But that's no excuse to do nothing. If you're a Christian, loving other people is not a "calling" you can patiently discover or wait for God to reveal to you. It's a direct, nonnegotiable command.

Some of us are called to go and be in the places where the biggest problems are. Some of us need to be there, working, helping, serving, not only on two-week trips in the summer but for years at a time, even lifetimes at a time. But some of us aren't supposed to do that now. It's not the right season. We're in school or providing for our family or training to go somewhere in the future.

But don't buy into the lie that "ministry" only happens overseas or during summer trips or on Tuesday evenings at small group or Sunday mornings at church. Ministry is about people in need, and those people are all around.

How can God use you to impact, change, affect, influence, love on, and meet the needs of the people all around you? What's holding you back? How can you break out of the fear and questions that keep you from "loving your neighbor as yourself"? (see Matthew 22:37–40).

That's what this book is all about: helping you ask and answer questions about yourself, your world, and your God that you might never have asked before—and then discover huge ways God can work in and through you to affect the people around you.

Lord, thank You for the opportunity to spend some serious time in Your Word, learning how to love others like You do. I pray for the discipline to stick with this devotional and allow Your Spirit to move and work in me. Be with me when I'm reading these words, affect me, change me, move me. Show me how I should be treating people differently in my life, how I can reach out and do a better job communicating Your love. These are big prayers, Lord. Help me not to get frustrated or disheartened, but to keep going, trusting that You're working in me to make me more like You. Amen.

PERSONAL INVENTORY QUESTIONS

I f we only listen or read, it's easy to just go through the motions. Writing stuff down helps make it stick. The "Notes to Self" sections are meant to help you record and remember your steps through this devotional. Think of them as big, yellow, sticky reminder notes. Jot down a phrase that sticks out or a verse that has struck you. Write the name of a person you've been praying for, or tape in their picture. Once a week you'll have room and time to work through what you've read, prayed, and experienced. Before we start, here's a "Personal Inventory" with a few questions to help establish a beginning point. At the end of these thirty days, we'll look at a similar survey to help you gauge your progress.

1) A new person arrives at my church or youth group. What is my response? I:

1. Introduce myself.
2. Make fun of their clothes.
3. Pretend I don't notice them.

2) I'm downtown with some friends and walk past a homeless person sitting on a bench. What am I feeling?

3) On the freeway ramp, I drive past a man flying a sign reading: "Hungry. Anything helps." I (do/don't) believe his sign. Then, I:

1. Pretend to try to find a new radio station.
2. Glance and make eye contact and then react as though I've been caught doing something I shouldn't.
3. Roll down the window and say hello.
4. Wish I had some food to help meet the need.

4) I'm feeling like God is asking me to do something really "uncomfortable." I:

1. Refuse to budge and put my head down, trusting it will "all go away soon."
2. Promise I'll pray about it, but forget about it when quiet time comes.
3. Seek counsel and find out if it's really the Lord's call on my life.

5) I just received a flier in the mail for a local homeless ministry. They're asking me to consider volunteering and/or helping financially. I:

1. Throw it away.
2. Put it in the drawer to look at next month.
3. Write a check so I don't feel guilty.
4. Write a check and find a time to deliver it while I'm volunteering at the mission.

6) What is my comfort zone? What are three things that make me uncomfortable?

7) Who is a person (or group of people) it's hard for me to feel like loving?

8) What kind of candy bar would be most difficult for me to give away?

PLEDGE

ARE YOU WILLING TO MAKE A COMMITMENT?

Lord, help me. I want to grow closer to You. That's why I'm doing this whole devotional anyway. Help me to grow, to realize what You want me to realize. Change my ideas about who I am, who others are, who You are, and what Your church is, so that I'll love others as You would have me love them.

I pledge here that I will try to find time every day to seek after You by working through this devotional. God, you know I'm busy and there are a ton of things competing for my time. Help me to have the discipline to do what I say I'm going to do, but also help me not to be too hard on myself when I fall short. Thanks for loving me so much. Draw me ever closer to You. Amen.

I, _____, pledge on this date, _____, to seek and earnestly desire to know God deeply and more fully. When this devotional asks me to do things that are challenging and outside my comfort zone, I will seek the Lord for the courage to step out and trust with everything I am that He will lead me where He wants me to go.

WEEK
ONE

LIFE ON THE STREETS

If God so loved us,
we also ought to love one another.

1 JOHN 4:11

As a bed, concrete is a real paradox—it has two conflicting qualities that add up to one really bad place to sleep. On the one hand, it is a gigantic sponge, soaking up all your body heat. If you're already cold, that's bad. On the other hand, concrete is rock hard. Not so spongelike. Good luck ever getting comfortable. Sleep is just one of the basics of staying alive most of us take for granted. Sam and I had to rethink hundreds of these basics, it seemed. Life on campus, life on the streets—it's shocking how much your life can change with just one decision.

At school, if I was hungry, all I needed to do was walk

to the cafeteria, swipe a card, and fill a tray with more food than I could possibly eat in one sitting. If I needed shelter, I had my own room and plenty of other options around town. And if I ever got stranded, I always had that handy plastic card. Living homeless, the best shelter I could hope for was the overhang from the entryway to a restaurant or coffee shop, or maybe a bridge if the weather got really bad. I kept napkins folded in my pockets, because who knew if I would have to go to the bathroom late at night when no public facilities were open and I had to use the bushes next to the street. I stuffed extra dinner rolls or pieces of bread in my pockets. To earn enough money for dinner, we would open up our guitar cases, sit on the ground at a busy crosswalk, and pray and sing our guts out. Sometimes it worked, and we were able to buy a meager meal from a nearby fast-food restaurant, but sometimes it didn't. When it didn't, we had two choices: go hungry or eat out of the trash.

Showering and cleanliness in general were distant memories. Sam and I once went five weeks without a shower. This might have been one of the reasons people treated us the way they did—usually with silent contempt. Hour after hour, person after person, we were ignored as we sat on the street corner, looking up at people walking past us. We discovered right away that generosity, when it came, was often from those who had very little with which to be generous.

One thing I learned on the streets was how easy it is to have an impact on someone's life when we're willing to take just a few moments out of our busy day, pray, and then figure out a way to help them.

To those who are in a lot of need, even the simplest things can have a profound impact. One cold morning, I bought a homeless woman a cup of coffee, and she literally burst into tears of gratitude. That's the kind of impact I'm talking about. Can you imagine being in a situation so desperate, so painful and lonely, that a stranger's offer to buy a cup of coffee would make you weep?

But as Christians, helping people is more than just kind acts toward others. We're called to love other people because God loves us (see 1 John 4:19). The real motivation for loving someone with a love that sees beyond what they look like, what they smell like, all the many ways they may be different from us, is to realize that God loved them so much He died to draw them to Himself.

Our responsibility is to step outside of ourselves, outside of our comfort zones, and serve someone else in order to help show them that love.

Question

Are you willing to step out of your comfort zone to help show the love of Christ?

Fact

In one year, 3.5 million people will be homeless in America.

> *You can't just walk in anyplace*
> *and ask for a drink or use the rest room.*
> JOHN HOWARD GRIFFIN, *BLACK LIKE ME*

God, I don't know if I'd be brave enough to give up everything, to really depend on You for absolutely every one of my needs. Maybe I don't have to take a step that big, but I know there are things that I'm holding on to that are keeping me from stepping off the ledge and following You. Give me the courage to do whatever You ask of me, regardless of what I have to give up. Amen.

WHAT FEAR?

I will not be afraid of many thousands of people
who have set themselves against me all around.

PSALM 3:6

In peace I will both lie down and sleep;
for you alone, O LORD, make me dwell in safety.

PSALM 4:8

S am and I were heading for the Martin Luther King Jr. Memorial Library in Washington DC, trying to find a place to sleep for the night. Several other homeless people usually slept around the large building, all of us thankful for the generous overhang that helped keep us dry.

We had just finished a long session of panhandling

without earning enough to eat dinner. As we walked we swapped stories of our childhood. The conversation made time pass and took our minds off our empty stomachs. For some reason, my stories centered on childhood fear— especially the terrors over the monster under my bed. Wow, I'd sure lost some sleep over that one!

"Don't worry, Mike," Sam told me as we approached the library. "You don't have a bed for monsters to live under anymore!"

Pale light was streaming out of the library windows, illuminating the figures of several sleeping men and women. Suddenly we noticed Tony. Tony was a few inches shorter than I was, but the tank top he wore revealed sweat glistening on powerful arms. Not a guy I would want to meet in a fight.

"Hey, Tony!" Sam called as we drew nearer. Tony didn't acknowledge our hello but instead moved more quickly toward us, expressionless in an eerie way.

"That's strange," I said, a little unnerved.

As we got closer, a concrete pillar came between us and Tony, and he disappeared behind it. Just as the concrete blocked my view, I saw Tony reach down toward his shoe. My stomach lurched into my throat.

Maybe it was the monster stories, or maybe I'd seen

too many action movies where the villain always has a knife hidden in his boot—but my adrenaline kicked into high gear. Two strides later, Tony lunged out from behind the pillar with a yell and swung a right hook straight at us. We both ducked, but it was unnecessary. Crazy Tony was just having some fun, trying to scare us. He didn't even have a knife. Our pulses were just getting back down to normal when Tony returned to pacing to and fro, screaming crazily into the night, his voice echoing off the concrete walls.

"You okay?" I asked Sam, still ready to fight.

"Yeah, nothing happened. You?"

"I'm good. Just shook up."

A woman nearby laughed. "Don't mind Tony," she said. "He's off-the-wall on crack right now."

After about ten minutes of trying to settle in for the night, Tony's eerie yelling drove us out. We ended up walking a mile through the city toward the church soup kitchen where we would eat in the morning.

When we could finally stretch out our bags, I laid awake staring at the three stars shining through the city lights, trying to calm my nerves. I noticed Sam was staring upward too.

"Still awake?" I asked.

"Yep," he said. "I was reading in Psalm 118 today..."

"Yeah?"

"Yeah. Verse six stuck out to me. 'The Lord is on my side; I will not fear. What can man do to me?'"

"Yeah?"

"Yeah. So why don't I feel any better?" Sam asked, only half joking.

"I was wondering the same thing," I said. "Maybe it's got something to do with the fact that I'm just saying the words, only halfheartedly believing them. I mean, let's say I really had to believe that God was going to watch out for me and keep me secure. Let's say I really believed that, when it matters, like right now when we're both freaked and can't sleep..."

"Hmm," Sam said. After a minute he spoke again. "It's easy to believe that God has laid you down to sleep in safety after you've locked the deadbolt. What about when you don't even have a door? Are you still so sure His promises are true?"

Question

Maybe God is asking you to do something a little strange, to step out of what's comfortable, surrender what's normal, and embrace what's different. God is strong enough to protect you and promises to be with you. But do you trust Him, even when you don't know what the outcome is going to be?

Fact

Half of the people on the streets have a serious substance abuse problem.

> *Lord, I know I'm supposed to be bold in You, but often, when I'm in a situation where I should step out and encourage someone or help meet a need, there's real fear in me. I don't mean to doubt You or Your promises; I'm not even sure where the fear comes from, which makes it hard to overcome it and get moving. Make the Scriptures come alive to me so that I will actually live with real trust in Your promises. Amen.*

SORRY YOU'RE HUNGRY

Let us not love in word or talk
but in deed and in truth.

1 JOHN 3:18

Before we hit the road, a friend had the perfect idea for staying fed. "Get an adorable puppy from the local animal shelter," he said. "Then sit next to the puppy with a sign that reads, 'Give us money for food or we'll eat the dog.'"

We laughed so hard over that idea that tears flowed down our cheeks. Okay, we never actually tried the puppy ploy. But maybe we should have...

I remember one hot lunch hour on a busy sidewalk in Washington DC. We were sweating heavily in the sun. People streamed past while we did our best to sing and play our guitars above the roar of the traffic.

Our cardboard sign said simply, "Hungry. Please donate for lunch." Then, smaller and more in the corner, it read, "Don't worry, tax write-off."

But no luck. No coins or bills in the guitar case. No leftovers. Nothing.

Sam finally stood up and announced that he was going to walk around the block and stretch his legs. I agreed to stay with the bags.

Sam crossed the street and waited to cross the next street. While waiting for the light to change, he asked the man in front of him a question. Though I didn't hear what was said, I could see the man turn to Sam, glare at him, and without a response, turn his back and move to position another person awkwardly between them. When Sam got back, he looked like he had been slapped in the face.

"Wow," I said as he sat down.

"Did you see that?" he asked, nodding across the street.

"Yeah, I did. What did you ask him that made him react that way?"

"I asked him what time it was."

We both sat for a while in silence. "Why do you think he responded that way?" Sam finally asked, voicing the confusion we both felt.

"I don't know," I said. "Probably the same reason everybody is passing by on their lunch break while we're obviously hungry here. We're judged instantly by what we look like or who people think we are, and that's enough to keep someone from ever acknowledging we even exist. Maybe it's time for us to get a puppy and a new sign!"

In frustration, I nudged our sign with my foot a little too hard and sent it skidding out into the foot traffic.

A man saw the sign getting trampled underfoot, so he grabbed it, read it, and handed it back.

"Tax write-off, huh?" he asked with a smirk.

"Yeah, it sure is!" Sam said. "We're definitely nonprofit!" We both nodded agreeably, thinking we might finally be in luck for lunch.

"Well, guys," the man said, taking off his cool sunglasses. "I'm sorry you're hungry. Really. But why don't you just go and get a job like everyone else you see walking around buying their own lunch?"

Without waiting for an answer, he shoved his sunglasses back on his face, nodded curtly, and continued on his way.

Back to nothing but empty, sweaty minutes.

"Remember Pamela?" I asked Sam, looking into the sea of people passing by.

"Yeah." He nodded. "We saw her a few weeks ago, right?"

"Yep. Remember that she didn't know what day it was, or where she was even at? She asked us on Sunday and then again on Monday what day it was, all the while thinking it was Tuesday."

Of course Sam and I could get jobs. We could work and be fed. Our homelessness was self-imposed—and, truthfully, so are some others' out here. But not Pamela's. Not hundreds of thousands of others' either. They can't function in ordinary society or they have no one to care for them, so they end up on the streets.

It's easy to say that we "love people" in a general sense, and then really not act like we love anybody at all when we're going about our days. Often we form an opinion of someone simply from the first interaction we have with them, or because of our interactions with people who are "like them." God's perspective is clear: Every person is an individual human being, created by God in His own image, and we're supposed to love not just with ideas and feelings but in deed and truth (see James 1:22; 2:14–17).

Fact

One-third of people on the streets have a serious mental illness.

Question

Think of a person you've tossed aside because of your pre-
conceived ideas of who they are or what they're like. How
can you engage that person through your actions?

> *Lord Jesus, thank You for what You've done for me.*
> *Please remind me of the ways that You've continued*
> *to accept me despite the many shortcomings I have.*
> *Help me to love other people with the same tenacity*
> *and honesty You show me. Help me to be a person*
> *who doesn't just talk about loving others, but actually*
> *does it. The difference is huge, so please give me the*
> *strength to live differently. Amen.*

DOMINICAN TRENCHES

> *There is neither Jew nor Greek, there is neither*
> *slave nor free, there is neither male nor female,*
> *for you are all one in Christ Jesus.*
>
> GALATIANS 3:28

The summer before my junior year in high school, I had an experience that radically affected my thinking and lifestyle. I had grown up in upper-middle-class America. Poverty was just a word to me, not a gut-wrenching reality. But as a new Christian that summer, I went on a short-term mission trip to the Dominican Republic with my church youth group. My wealth-oriented way of thinking was about to get hung out to dry after an intense spin cycle.

Our project was to build a baseball field for the students at a Christian school. One day during our construction work, when the typical Caribbean midday downpour began, all of us were worried that we wouldn't be able to complete a section of trench and foundation on time. After lunch, my new Dominican friend Manuel and I stood looking out at the slowly flooding fields and decided to do something radical. Even though he knew almost no English, and I even less Spanish, we still managed to communicate a plan.

Ignoring the downpour, we ran out into the field, grabbed shovels and pickaxes, and went back to work.

Ten minutes later I was soaked, mud was up to my knees, and sweat stung my eyes...but we started singing. I was singing in English and Manuel was singing in Spanish, but it was the same song, so it worked. Harmony, in fact, demands difference. Two of the same note doesn't make harmony.

Up to that moment, I had only noticed our differences, what kept us apart:

I was white. Manuel was black.

I was rich. Manuel was poor.

I spoke English. Manuel spoke Spanish.

I was from America. Manuel was from the Dominican Republic.

I had an education. Manuel didn't.

I had an unlimited future. Manuel really didn't.

All that stuff was there, present and available for either one of us to use as an excuse to push the other person away and draw insurmountable lines and distance between us.

But with our worship in that mud-filled trench, I was seeing something new, something important. In worship of our Lord, in harmony of song, harmony of pickaxes and shovels, harmony of worship, harmony of sweat and rain and mud, Manuel and I were one. That is one of the most important gifts of the gospel of Christ. Old, obvious differences that keep people apart and in conflict just crumble and disappear.

That's what Paul wrote about: "All are one." God sees every one of us exactly the same: as people in need of Him. That truth, indifferent to socioeconomic status, education, race, gender, or future potential describes every human on the face of the planet. And those who follow after Christ are His body, the church, and though there are different parts (eyes, ears, Dominicans, Americans), the need for unity in Christ far outweighs the differences between us. Looking back, I see how much that awakening in the Dominican trenches changed the way I thought about people in my hometown, the people I passed on the streets every day, and those who I considered to be "different" than me.

I think that's what redemption is all about—watching things that once were a certain way change to become more in line with what God really wants.

Question

Think of a time when you bonded with someone who seemed to be your complete opposite. How did it feel to find out that you could feel so close to someone so different from you?

Lord, thank You for overcoming all of the differences that I am so quick to highlight. Thanks for being a God who makes the differences simply fade away. Help me to remember this truth today as person after person crosses my path, and I find myself constantly examining them, critiquing them, and comparing them to me. Let Your love cover the differences and bring us together. Help me to encourage others toward this as well, and to stand up for what I know to be true. Amen.

GOOSE-BUMP PREACHER

*Religion that is pure and undefiled before God,
the Father, is this: to visit orphans and
widows in their affliction, and to keep
oneself unstained from the world.*

JAMES 1:27

met Norm, a toothless sixty-year-old, under a bridge in Portland one afternoon when the heavy air smelled of booze and urine, and we were all sitting around waiting for the rescue mission to open its doors for dinner. Norm usually wore a baseball cap, and his face was worn and weathered. Norm told me he actually had two jobs. At night he was what he called a "trash treasure hunter." He followed a carefully planned route that took him around the city dumpsters. Usually he came up with something to dull his hunger. But Norm said he'd also found real treasures. He told of finding diamond rings, Rolex watches, many pairs of gold-rimmed glasses, and even the occasional twenty-dollar bill accidentally shuffled into the trash between restaurant receipts.

"Yep," he said, proudly showing me a row of impressive watches on his arm. "There's a lot of treasure being thrown away every night in this city."

Norm's second job was lawn maintenance at a mansion in the hills above town. The woman who owned the place paid him well. Made him lunch too, he said.

"How long have you been doing that, Norm?" I asked, intrigued.

"Oh, about ten years or so. Every week to two weeks. It's a great job. I was flying a sign that said, 'Will work for food,' and I really meant it. She stopped, asked me if I wanted a job doing yard work, and, well, that's how it started."

Norm represented one of the many interesting types of people on the streets. He didn't have a college education and had worked minimum-wage jobs most of his life. He was one of the only sober men under the bridge that day.

Later, we were sitting in the rescue mission chapel waiting for the service to begin when Mr. Peterson, a flustered-looking member of the mission's staff, rushed to the front of the chapel.

"It seems our chapel service this evening has decided not to show. I don't really have anything to say either, but does anybody want to share why they're thankful to God today?"

After a moment, one person began clapping.

Then a man near the front stood up to say how thankful he was that it hadn't rained in two days. Next, a woman stood to say she was thankful for the dinner coming that evening.

Just as the man at the front looked like he was about to say something, Norm raised his hand. He held a tattered Bible open as he began to speak.

"Everybody, my name is Norm. And there are two things I would like to say. The first is from James 1:27, in which it is written, 'Religion that is pure and undefiled before God, the Father, is this: to visit orphans and widows in their affliction, and to keep oneself unstained from the world.' Now, not very many people want to come visit us in our affliction, in our poverty, as is obvious because our chapel program canceled on us."

Then Norm turned to look directly at Mr. Peterson. "Mr. Peterson, thank you for the work you do here. You do a lot of good for all of us out there on the streets. But there are a lot of people who read this Bible same as you and I do. Why ain't more of them down here to visit 'orphans and widows in their affliction'? Some of us are orphans and widows, and we're all down-and-out, so I ask you, where are all the Christians?"

With a final nod, Norm sat down, not really expecting any response. Several people said loud amens while others clapped their approval.

I looked over at Sam and whispered, "Good question. I was wondering the same thing!"

Missions around the country are able to continue functioning because of the large amounts of financial support they receive every year, but they need volunteers too. However, for most of us, a financial contribution is all that we're willing to give (if we're willing to give anything). There's a reason James says "visit" those who are in need, those who are outcasts, those who are "thrown away" by society. There's something incredible that happens when you actually go to the places of deep need in the world. You feel connected to the need, even responsible to help change it. Experience makes you want to make more of a difference because you discover that these "thrown away" people are treasure in God's eyes.

Question

What does "visiting" mean for you? Maybe it's just a conversation. Or maybe it's volunteering at a local homeless shelter.

> *Christian love, either towards God*
> *or towards man, is an affair of the will.*
> C. S. LEWIS, *MERE CHRISTIANITY*

Lord Jesus, You left heaven to come down and be with people here on this earth. Thank You for doing that, for leaving heaven behind to have a relationship with me. Help me to do the same thing, to not just support from afar, but actually go where the needs are, spend time with those who are hurting, make friends with the outcasts. Give me the courage to "visit" these people. I don't know how, Lord. But You do. Show me. Amen.

GOOD WORKS?

> *Let your manner of life be worthy*
> *of the gospel of Christ.*
>
> PHILIPPIANS 1:27

You might be getting a little uneasy with the emphasis I'm putting on the action, or works, part of our walk with Christ. Maybe you feel like I'm swinging too far toward the "what we do" side at the expense of the "where we place our faith" side of the balance.

I'd understand if you feel this way. But let me clarify my position. The basis of anyone's salvation—how you and I get right with God and have our sins forgiven—is their faith in Jesus Christ, God's Son. His work on the cross on our behalf was to die in our place. Belief in Christ is what saves us and draws us into new life with God. Scripture is clear that "whoever believes in Him should not perish but have eternal life" (John 3:16).

We don't have to do a single good deed to get saved—and that includes buying one cup of coffee for one shivering street person. But once our new life has begun, what should come next? How will our new life look as our faith becomes more a part of our days?

That's where what we do matters—a lot!

Taking the plunge to believe in Jesus is the first of many steps in the lifelong journey of faith. And with these pages I'm challenging you to press ahead in this journey with Jesus—because getting saved is easy (Jesus did all the work, right?), but doing the work of faith is hard. And yet that is what every follower of Christ is called to do!

Look at some of the ways the apostle Paul described this lifestyle and the visible good works that result from faith in Christ:

> We are his workmanship, created in
> Christ Jesus for good works, which God
> prepared beforehand, that we should
> walk in them. (Ephesians 2:10)

> They are to do good, to be rich in good
> works, to be generous and ready to share.
> (1 Timothy 6:18)

Show yourself in all respects to be a
model of good works. (Titus 2:7)

All Scripture is breathed out by
God...that the man of God may be com-
petent, equipped for every good work.
(2 Timothy 3:16–17)

Work out your own salvation with fear
and trembling, for it is God who works in
you, both to will and to work for his good
pleasure. (Philippians 2:12–13)

Paul was adamant about pushing other followers of
Christ to make their faith real through what they *did*.
Paul's idea of faith *required* acting it out, living in a certain
way. If this "faith lived out loud" was so important to Paul,
it's safe to say that we should seriously consider how
we're acting out our faith today in our world.

The good news is we don't have to live out our faith
in our strength alone. After we make that first step to follow after Christ, He actually begins to live through us. In
Galatians 2:20 Paul says, "It is no longer I who live, but
Christ who lives in me." Don't know how to serve God

and help others? No worries! God says He will live through you, and that means He will inform your thoughts, words, and actions. As you follow Him and ask Him to show Himself through you, He will open your eyes to the needs around you, and good works will become a lifestyle.

Question

What are some ways you can live your faith out loud like Paul describes in the previous Bible verses? Do them today.

> *God, thank You for sending Your Son, Jesus, to this world. You told us through the prophets that You love us, but then You showed us Your love by being with us, dying on the cross, and then getting up again on the third day. Lord, help me to show people my faith in the decisions I make, in the conversations I have, in everything I do. Live in me so that my faith will be real. Amen.*

1.7

ACTION DAY #1

*Jesus promises a life in which we
increasingly have to stretch our hands and be
led into places where we would rather not go.*

HENRI NOUWEN, *IN THE NAME OF JESUS*

O kay, here we are—the first day where I give you practical recommendations for activities to actually go out and *do*. I'm excited that you've made it this far in the devotional. But remember, you've made it this far after agreeing you were willing to do more than simply read this book. It's time to put your faith in action in a real and challenging way.

The things I'm going to recommend below may well seem difficult, inconvenient, or downright strange. But we need to remember that it was probably difficult, inconvenient, and downright strange for Jesus Christ, God

Himself, to come down out of heaven and spend thirty years here on this earth, then be crucified and resurrected. God first loved you, and then through His Word, He commands you to "go and do likewise" and "love your neighbor as yourself" (see Luke 10:25–37).

So here are a few ideas:

OPTION 1: GRANOLA BARS AND BOTTLED WATER

Here's an easy idea. Buy bottled waters and the same number of soft granola bars (some homeless people don't have teeth). Then tape a granola bar to each bottle. Put them in a cardboard box or milk crate in the back of your car (or your parents' car). When you see someone flying a sign on the freeway on-ramp or off-ramp, offer them one of the bottles of water with the granola bar attached. On a long, hot afternoon, one of these little gifts will change someone's day.

OPTION 2: CLOTHING DRIVE

Most of us have more clothes than we even realize. Go to your closet, stand in front of it for a while, and be honest with yourself. Take out all of the clothes that you have not worn in the past year (I'll bet there are a ton that you're holding on to "just in case," but that you'll never actually wear). Maybe go to a few neighbors and ask them if they'd be willing to donate an old winter coat or any other clothing they don't want anymore. Wash, dry, and iron these clothes just as if you were going to wear them tonight and wanted to look good. Then take them to a local shelter and donate them so they can be distributed to those who are in real need. Or if you're feeling up to the task, take your excess useful clothing to a downtown area and offer it to some of the homeless. Don't do this alone. Instead, try to get several other people to go with you; you'll be safer, and you'll make an even bigger impact.

OPTION 3: BAG OF GROCERIES

Go to a local grocery store, grab a shopping cart, and go up and down the aisles throwing in the things that *you* would like to eat. Items that don't need to be refrigerated are best. Maybe it's peanut butter and jelly with a loaf of bread, a few bags of potato chips, maybe some chocolate chip cookies, definitely some fruit or some canned vegetables. Purchase the groceries and see if you can fit them all in one paper sack. Get one with handles if possible to make it easier to carry. Then, drive to a nearby downtown area, and when you see someone who is homeless, offer them the bag of groceries. Or maybe you already know a family in need. Unexpected gifts are often the most moving.

Whatever you do, remember to keep the focus on the people you're doing it for (not your own good deeds). That focus means, for example, taking the time whenever possible to connect personally with the man or woman you're helping. A little eye contact and conversation goes a long way. You might also offer to pray for them, or with them, depending on what they want. Let them know that there is a God who intimately cares for them and wants them to know Him, and that He is the reason you're trying to help others.

Pray hard for the Lord to work in and through you so you can accomplish His purposes while you're out doing these things. To help you get started, pray these words:

Lord, thank You for saving me and bringing me close to You. Help me bring this gift of Your love to others who don't know You yet. I want to be Your representative. I want to do Your will, so please lead and guide me as I step out in faith, out of my comfort zone, forgetting myself and my selfish desires in order to serve someone else. Remind me again and again today, Lord, that I love others because You first loved me. Please protect me as I do this and also prepare the hearts of those I will meet today, so that my actions and words will actually be understood and appreciated. Thy will be done, Lord! Amen.

NOTES TO SELF

a. Something God showed me this week:

_____

_____

_____

_____

_____

_____

b. A question I've pondered this week:

_____

_____

_____

_____

_____

_____

_____

c. Someone I met this week I want to remember:

d. A decision I've made this week to change how I live:

e. More notes to self:

THE NEW BRYCE

If anyone is in Christ, he is a new creation.
The old has passed away; behold, the new has come.

2 CORINTHIANS 5:17

O ne warm evening, I sat out on a high fire escape on the side of the Denver Rescue Mission with a guy named David. David was a "pipeliner"—fresh off the street and in the first stages of rehab.

While we sat there looking out at the city lights, David seemed to be wavering. He asked me how in the world rehabilitation was supposed to work anyway, especially when for the last twenty years of his life, everyone he knew and everything he did had been defined by addiction.

As David spoke, a big realization slapped me in the face. Rehabilitation requires more than a decision to "just say no." The growth, the change, the work necessary were beyond David's resolve or even the mission's award-winning rehabilitation program. The path of rehabilitation is a long and difficult journey. Many drop out. Many who don't relapse later. The deep changes of recovery cry out for revolution, for the true, new life that God offers in Jesus Christ.

I remember Bryce, a guy I worked with in a mission kitchen in Santa Barbara. The first time I met him he was singing an old Led Zeppelin tune at the top of his lungs and working the dish sprayer with a vengeance in the cleanup line.

Bryce was forty-five years old and had been a methamphetamine addict for close to ten years. He had owned and operated a successful business for nearly twenty years, but the money from his business had enabled his addiction to start, develop, and then pretty much destroy him. At the end, he had lost his business, his marriage, his family—and almost his life.

Rehab at the rescue mission was his last hope. One time when we were stacking trays, he told me, "I fully expect to be dead within the year if I drop out of this program."

I was shocked by Bryce's honesty. "How's it going so far?" I asked.

"One day at a time, right?" he said with a wink. "I'm clean and I'm still here."

About a week later, Bryce caught me off-guard with a question:

"Do you know much about Jesus?"

I was surprised because the conversation had instantly jumped from surfing to Jesus.

"Well, sure," I answered.

Bryce chose his words carefully. "Do you believe He can really change someone's life?"

I stopped washing plates and turned to face him. "Absolutely," I said. "I believe He's the only one who can, actually."

"Huh," Bryce said, thinking. "What I've heard here is that all I need to do is believe, and I'm saved."

"That's true. Just believe in Him and your sins are forgiven."

"Just like that?"

"Jut like that." I thought for a minute, and then added, "But you know, that's just the start. Christianity is a journey. One that lasts your whole life. It's like when you married your wife. You both said, 'I do,' and bam, you were married. But you still had a lot to learn, a lot to discover, and a lot of stumbles along the way. Believing in Christ for the first time is like the first step in the journey of marriage. Both last for the rest of your life, but you have to make a decision first. Saying 'I do' just starts things off."

Time passed, and I lost track of Bryce. But about a year later I was down on the streets near the mission when a man ran up. "Mike? Is that you?" he asked.

It was Bryce—big smile, freshly shaved, hair cut, carrying a backpack, wearing a button-down shirt tucked into khaki pants. What a transformation!

Bryce had made that decision to start walking on the journey of Christianity, and some incredible changes had occurred. Now, after graduating from the mission, he was working on getting his master's degree in drug and alcohol counseling.

After a few minutes Bryce said he had to go. He needed to head back to the mission for a class. He was the teacher.

As he walked away, I yelled after him, "Hey, Bryce, do you believe Jesus can really change someone's life?"

He turned around, thought for a second, and said, "I'm still here and I'm still clean." With a wink he walked into the mission.

Question

Do you believe that the Lord can completely change a person as He draws them closer to Him? Identify one person you interact with for whom it is hard to believe this transformation is even possible. How can you encourage them along in the transformation process?

Fact

In 2004 nearly 14,500 people graduated from rescue-mission-based programs.

> *Lord God Almighty, You can change a person completely. Thank You for promising to change me if I give myself up to You and start walking the journey to become more like You. Help me to realize how complete a transformation You are able to bring in my life—in everyone's life. I don't want to ever look at someone as if they are beyond Your redemption. Thank You for wanting everyone to be saved and never turning anyone away. Teach me to love people that way! Amen.*

DINNER AND A MOVIE

Be doers of the word, and not hearers only.

JAMES 1:22

A heavy rain was drenching Portland, and Sam and I were soaked through. When you're homeless and dirty, being wet makes everything worse. Especially the smell. You wouldn't believe how much worse a filthy shirt smells when it's wet. Think dirty wet dog to the stench power of ten, and you'll start to get what I'm saying.

But on this day we needed to walk, rain or no, because we'd gotten word of a free all-you-can-eat dinner and movie being offered at a downtown church. Turns out, we didn't have dinner plans. (The truth is, the dinner, if it materialized, would be the first food we had that day.)

Along the way we came across a couple of other homeless guys who were wearing plastic garbage bags and offered us two to help stay dry. The bags already had holes cut in them for a head and two arms.

Sam and I thanked them and asked if they had heard of this "Dinner and a Movie" too. Soon all four of us were walking toward the church, drawn by the promise of food and a warm, dry room to relax in. The simplest things can have such a profound impact when you're in need...

Like a few days earlier, when we had a chance to be the ones on the giving end: Sam and I had wrapped up a particularly good streak of panhandling, so we decided to buy burritos and hand them out to other homeless guys we encountered on our way back to our bridge for the night. I sat down next to a disheveled-looking man, struck up a conversation, and handed him a burrito. After about five minutes he stopped chewing long enough to thank me.

As he talked, his eyes welled up with tears. "This is the first conversation I've had in about a week. It gets so lonely out here sometimes."

He told me I'd completely changed his day.

With a five-minute conversation and two-dollar burrito? Imagine what a full meal and a movie could mean to people scraping by out on the streets.

At the church we were met by a smiling guy who

handed each of us a towel and told us to dry ourselves off a bit. Then we lined up for dinner.

Pretty soon the room was packed with about one hundred people, all talking loudly, enjoying lasagna, salad, and breadsticks.

"How's the food, guys?" Sam and I said as we sat down across from two guys we hadn't met before.

"Awesome, man," one said through a mouthful. The guy next to him agreed. "Best meal I've had in almost a month. The salad's even fresh!"

When I had eaten enough to finally give my stomach something to work at digesting, I began looking around the room. That's when I saw some words painted on the wall above the food line:

> Be doers of the word, and not hearers only.
> (James 1:22)

Earlier that afternoon in the Portland library, I read an article by a man describing a scene from his church in Germany in the early 1940s. The church was located next to some railroad tracks that ran into a Nazi concentration camp. When the trains came by during services, church members would sing louder, the man said, in order to drown out the screams from the prisoners onboard who knew they were en route to certain death.

I know there's a big difference between helping Jews in the 1940s and helping homeless people today. But ignoring suffering is never the right thing to do. The "Dinner and a Movie" Christians chose to *do* something that helped warm and feed hundreds of people every week. That seems like being "doers" of the Word to me.

Question

What's one way you can *do* something from the Word today in your life? Maybe it involves a friend, a family member, or a person you hardly know. Be open to it, and let the Lord lead!

Lord, help me to be a "doer" of the Word, rather than just a "hearer." Forgive me for the times I've ignored suffering people instead of being willing to act out the love that I profess. Show me ways I can seek justice and show mercy. Give me Your eyes to see so I will be concerned about the things that are important to You. Amen.

LITTLE JOHNNY

And if anyone would sue you and take your tunic,
let him have your cloak as well. If anyone forces
you to go one mile, go with him two miles.

MATTHEW 5:40–41

After our first week in San Diego, Sam and I decided to vacate the downtown area and head out to Ocean Beach. We heard from several street people that "OB," as it was lovingly referred to, was much more friendly and welcoming to street people like us.

The quaint little town had a true Southern California feel, with its laid-back, flip-flop-wearing residents, that instantly made us feel welcome. The main strip ended at a small park area where most of the homeless people would hang out together in the evenings. Our first night there we met quite a few friendly people.

As we went around shaking hands and introducing ourselves, a man named Johnny stepped up to introduce himself with a gaping, toothless smile. The purple bandanna stretched Rambo-style across the middle of his forehead was soaked through with sweat. Instead of letting the handshake drop once it was finished, Johnny drew each of us into a great big bear hug and squeezed a tight welcome. He reeked of alcohol.

"Don't mind him," a lady sitting on a concrete wall said through a thick cloud of cigarette smoke. "He means no harm. Just loves new faces."

"Great to see you guys!" Johnny nearly yelled as he sat back down next to the woman. "Hey, you guys had any dinner yet?"

We shook our heads no as we set down our packs with a sigh. "Me neither!" Johnny yelled, bursting into laughter. He was the only one still laughing after Sam's and my courtesy laugh had ended. This guy was a character! The lady next to him told him to knock it off and smacked him, only half kidding.

We sat at the end of the road watching the sun sink lower into the crashing Pacific Ocean, chatting intermittently with our new OB friends. We talked about the best places to camp, the best spots to panhandle, and areas to stay away from. The kindness and openness of the home-less community always astounded us. It was like these men and women considered the streets of OB their home, and just as you or I would warmly welcome a visitor with open arms, they welcomed us with insight and know-how that would have taken us months to gather.

Within an hour we knew the lay of the land and had learned about a few places serving free meals a couple days a week. Johnny also told us about a great place to lay out our sleeping bags not more than a half mile down the beach.

After buying a jar of peanut butter and a package of tortillas, Sam and I headed off to the spot near the cliffs that Johnny recommended. We sat atop our bags, the stars twinkling above and the city lights shining behind us, the waves crashing so close we felt the mist. We each feasted on at least four peanut-butter corn tortillas, and then turned in for the night.

Before we fell asleep, though, we carefully wrapped the remaining tortillas and peanut butter in a plastic sack and stuffed it between our packs for safekeeping during the night.

Around 3 a.m. I remember hearing a loud, familiar laugh in the middle of a strange dream.

The next morning, at first light, Sam and I awoke almost simultaneously. I lay there in my sleeping bag not sure what was worse, staying in a cold, damp sleeping bag or stepping into a cold, foggy world.

As Sam and I debated the pluses and minuses of each, we noticed with shock that our bag of food was no longer in the place we had stashed it the night before.

We both sat up, driven out into the cold by our curiosity and growing anger. You don't mess with a homeless man's food. As we surveyed the nearby landscape, we didn't have to look very far to see somebody lying against the cliffs.

We quickly jumped out of our bags and sprinted the thirty yards to where Johnny lay, snoring contentedly. The sight that we saw when we neared would have been humorous—if it hadn't been our stash of supplies, that is. The peanut-butter jar lay on its side, a line of ants entering to devour what little was left. The tortillas were completely gone, though crumbs were scattered all over the sleeping Johnny.

"Hey, Johnny," I said, quite frustrated and not really trying to hide it.

Nothing.

"Johnny. Wake up," Sam said, also angry.

Johnny stirred and slowly realized what was going on. When his eyes focused on Sam and me standing above him, he sat upright quickly and began looking around.

"Johnny, man," I said. "You ate all our food! Why'd you do that?" I picked up the peanut-butter jar for effect and looked to Johnny for an answer.

Suddenly Johnny burst into tears and started apologizing. That wasn't really what I was expecting. Come to think of it, I don't know what I was expecting.

"Oh, no," Johnny said between his tears. "I can't believe I did that. Guys, I'm so sorry. I was a little off last night, and, well, I was hungry when I saw the bag and didn't even think about it. I'm so sorry." The tears were thick and real, and completely knocked me over.

Why was I so upset with Johnny? He was hungry and we had food. We would have gladly given him some of the tortillas if he'd asked, but it was the idea that he took them from us that had made me mad in the first place. Now he was apologizing and truly felt sorry about it.

My anger dissipated as I thought about it more and realized how easy it would be for Sam and me to get another jar of peanut butter and package of tortillas. Sure, it would take a few hours of panhandling, but if it helped Johnny when he was hungry...

It's hard to let yourself be injured for the sake of Christ. I never much like reading that verse in Matthew. The first thing I think of is *my* rights and how they've been trampled on. It would seem, though, that humility is more important than "my rights."

If someone takes your peanut butter, give them your tortillas as well.

Question

It's easy to demand our rights when we feel that we've been wronged, isn't it? But sometimes we need to put our "rights" aside and serve the person we think has wronged us. Make a resolution to do this, and you will give glory to Christ.

> *My role is to receive you with hospitality*
> *and to let you go with peace.*
> THOMAS MERTON, *WISDOM OF THE DESERT*

Lord, I want my life to be fair, but justice is different in Your eyes than in mine. I only see how things affect me, but You see everything and know everyone's needs. Help me to know when I should forget my own rights and just be humble. Give me the strength to serve and love the person who is trying to take something that is rightfully mine. Let it be to Your glory, Lord. Amen.

ART OF ADDICTION

There came a man full of leprosy. And when he saw Jesus,
he fell on his face and begged him, "Lord, if you will,
you can make me clean." And Jesus stretched
out his hand and touched him.

LUKE 5:12–13

A utumn in Santa Barbara typically brings warm, sunny days and brisk, foggy evenings. Downtown, all along State Street, people who drive Ferraris and shop at Saks mingle with a homeless population that grows as people drift in from harsher climates in the north. And on Thursday evenings, students from Westmont College join the scene to bring food and conversation to the needy.

The student-led program, called Bread of Life, provides a home-cooked meal (typically spaghetti or lasagna, bread, salad, pie for dessert, and juice to wash it all down) for forty or fifty homeless people who gather expectantly at seven. The dinner is only part of the evening, though, and after the food is gone, an hour or so is spent just hanging out, shooting the breeze, talking about the weather or sports or politics or faith in Christ or whatever.

That hour is critical. You see, it's not only about the food, but it's also about the person who is hungry.

On one of those nights I met Art. He was so drunk he could hardly stand, but several of us decided to hang out with him and get to know him a little bit better. As he ate, slowly some clarity returned to his eyes and his speech became less slurred. For forty minutes the students heard tales, stories, and truths from the harsh existence that was Art's life on the streets. Our simple willingness to listen caused Art to burst into tears at several points. So did the gift of a new blanket from a nearby thrift store that a student handed him after learning his had been stolen.

But as Art sobered up, the painkilling effect of the alcohol faded too. Having just finished his lasagna, Art rose from the planter on which he was sitting, took one step, and toppled to the ground screaming.

We knelt beside him, asking him what was wrong.

"My leg, my leg!" Art groaned, writhing in pain.

After futile attempts to help him, we called an ambulance.

Once the paramedics had him on a stretcher, they cut Art's pants from his ankles to his knees, then cut off his socks too.

Midprocedure, the stench forced the paramedic to take two steps back in disgust. Then maggots began falling onto the pavement.

Maggots were eating Art's leg.

Needless to say, most of us were appalled. What could possibly have led to this? Why was a human being—made in the image of almighty God—living life on the streets, swimming in alcohol, and being eaten alive by maggots?

I could tell you that it's sin—Art's sin for choosing to drink instead of dealing with his problems, his parents' sin for abandoning him when he was a child, the local church's sin for not finding ways to engage the homeless community in a deeper way, the sin of the people who pass him by every day without a second thought.

That is all true. Sin caused Art to be in the place he was. But sometimes there are things in this life, things in this world, that are so messed up, so hard to deal with, so hard to look at, that just slapping down a simple three-letter word and walking away seems a mockery. You can be right and still heartless, you know.

When Christ walked on this earth, rarely did He ask how or why about a person's situation.

Look at how He responds to the leper in Luke 5. Lepers, you know, where the social outcasts of Jesus' day. They were unclean by Jewish law. You didn't look at them, didn't talk to them, and certainly didn't touch them. Besides, everyone "knew" that their bodies were rotting away for one reason: sin.

But Jesus acknowledges the person behind the leprosy. He doesn't ask how or why; He just heals the man's disease.

I saw Art a couple of weeks ago as I walked past the library. He was drunk again, but at least he still had two good legs.

"Hey, man!" Art cried. "You're one of the Westmont kids who comes down and hangs out with us every week, aren't you?!"

"Yeah, I am," I said, smiling.

"Man, you guys are awesome. Thank you, man. Thank you."

Question

Ministry is about more than just meeting needs; it's about connecting with the person in need. What does that mean for you in your life? Think of one person you will intentionally interact with differently because of this idea.

Lord, thank You for seeing past my sin. Remind me that You came to fix what is broken and heal the sick, and that I should want to do the same. Forgive me for the times that I look at suffering people and think their situation is hopeless and forget that You can fix anything. Help me to love others the way You do. Amen.

BERKELEY AFTERNOON

So then, as we have opportunity,
let us do good to everyone, and especially
to those who are of the household of faith.

GALATIANS 6:10

One Sunday morning in Berkeley, Sam and I visited a church we'd seen the day before. We were early, but as people filed in, we noticed that we still had plenty of room—a ten-foot margin on all sides—even though worshipers had packed the rest of the sanctuary by the opening hymn. That might have been self-defense on their part, though. At this point in our journey, we'd gone nearly five weeks without a shower. We didn't smell too fresh.

Okay, we reeked.

But still...

Funny how what Jesus smelled like is never mentioned in the New Testament. Sure, they had fragrant spices in those days, myrrh and expensive perfumes and all that. But do you think Jesus' fishermen friends kept a few bottles of cologne on their boats? Do you think Jesus packed shampoo and conditioner for his disciples for their treks through Samaria? What about antibacterial soap? I think not.

So, there we sat—lots of people around us, but no one close, everyone at a safe distance. We stuck out like a broken toenail on the body of Christ. When Sam and I walked out of the church, not a single person had extended a handshake or said hello or even nodded in our direction.

You may be thinking, *Didn't they have greeters at the church?* Yes, they did. There were people standing at the doors when we walked in, but, more importantly, there were two hundred or so potential "greeters" in the pews all around us. In any church, biblical commands to show kindness and hospitality to strangers aren't optional. Why should they be delegated?

After the service, we walked away from the church feeling dejected. Add pangs of hunger, and our day wasn't looking too bright. But we had only gone a block when a man from the church came running after us.

"Hey there, guys!" he said with a grin.

"Hey!" Sam and I both replied, curious.

"I'm just about to head back to my house for lunch with another friend. We were wondering if you'd be interested in coming along? You can shower up, do some laundry, grab some food, and then be on your way."

I stared at Sam in disbelief. Wow! What a turnaround!

"Are you serious?" Sam asked, amazed.

The guy laughed a little and nodded. "My name's Joe. C'mon. I'll show you where my car is." When we got to his Toyota, he popped the trunk and told us to throw our packs in. "Let me run in and grab my friend, and then we'll head over to my place. My wife's gone on a trip to the East Coast, so we'll have a guy's afternoon."

Minutes later, Sam and I were taking turns cleaning up in Joe's shower and putting his washing machine to good use. Then we stood around his stove, cooking up some delicious bratwurst.

While the steam rose and an incredible aroma filled the room, we got to know one another. Joe and his friend Mark had met in college and now lived in the same neighborhood.

I asked Joe why he had run after us that morning.

"Thought you might be hungry!" Joe said.

"Huh," I said, not completely satisfied. I guess my face betrayed my feelings.

"Actually," Joe said, more thoughtfully, "the real reason is something I read yesterday in Galatians: 'So then, as we have opportunity, let us do good to everyone, and especially to those who are of the household of faith.'"

Then it was Mark's turn. "I've got to apologize to you guys. I thought Joe was crazy when he told me that he felt like we should ask you guys to lunch. Off his rocker, you know? I was worried you guys would mug us and leave us for dead. But it's like what I read in Hebrews this morning: 'Let us consider how to stir up one another to love and good works' (10:24). Joe, you were doing that this morning, even though I thought you were crazy."

As we ate, Sam and I shared stories of our travels with Mark and Joe as we would with old friends. Joe's willingness to seize the opportunity to "do good" had closed the distance we'd experienced earlier.

Friendship can do that.

Friendship along with a hot shower, honest conversation, and steaming bratwurst does it even better.

Question

One of the best ways to "stir up one another to love and good works" is for you to love and do good works. What are some good deeds that you can do today in your world? Who are some people you can show real love to?

Quote

We talk about leading a different kind of life, but we also have ready explanations for not being really different.

DALLAS WILLARD, *THE SPIRIT OF THE DISCIPLINES*

Lord, thank You for accepting me unconditionally. And thank You for sending Jesus, who wasn't afraid to hang out with outcasts and sinners. God, I am afraid to do that because all I can see is how different those people are from me. Show me how to have the love and acceptance that Jesus has, Father. Teach me to be brave enough to not only meet people's physical needs, but offer friendship and relationship too. Amen.

WHAT'S A NEIGHBOR?

> *"Which of these three, do you think,*
> *proved to be a neighbor to the man who fell among*
> *the robbers?" He said, "The one who showed him mercy."*
> *And Jesus said to him, "You go, and do likewise."*
>
> LUKE 10:36–37

You've probably walked by some less-than-appealing member of humanity on the streets and felt torn about your responsibility to respond. Should you...stop, talk, buy a meal, give money, take them home with you? Or keep walking and let someone else "deal with them"?

I bet you feel the same tug of conscience when you see the desperate needs in developing countries portrayed on TV. Or maybe simply when you're out with friends. You notice someone outside your circle who's obviously in need of friendship, of community...and you have a choice to make.

Congratulations! What you're wrestling with is an issue that has perplexed great minds—even great Christian minds—since Cain asked God, "Am I my brother's keeper?" The question is: How responsible are we for meeting the needs of others, especially "outsiders" who appear to add little or no value to the community?

Guess it's no surprise that the best minds of Jesus' day hit Him with the same biggie. You might remember the story:

A lawyer wants to justify himself before Jesus, so he asks what he should do to inherit eternal life. Jesus responds with the commandments, "Love God, and love your neighbor."

The man isn't satisfied, so he asks, "Who is my neighbor?" He wants to make sure he's doing it right, wants to make himself feel better. *Who* should he be loving? Certainly not everybody. That's impossible. *Who* is his neighbor? Who is he "required" to love?

Jesus answers the man's question with a story we all know: the story of the Good Samaritan. A story similar to an evening I had not too long ago.

My friend Dave and I were downtown, in a big hurry

to meet some friends for dinner, when we noticed a woman sitting on the sidewalk, her feet just inches from the traffic speeding past. I tried to make eye contact with her, then tried an out-of-breath "Hey there!" as we passed. But no response.

We were a bit farther up the sidewalk when I suddenly had a deep sense that I had missed something back there. But should we turn around? We were late for dinner, and obviously she hadn't responded to my attempted hello.

Go back?

Go on?

I bet you know what I'm talking about.

Tough, isn't it?

This time, I did go back. What turned me around was sudden clarity (which doesn't happen to me much) that I could choose to be a neighbor to this woman or choose not to be.

Dave and I approached her carefully.

"Ma'am?" I said, softly, trying not to startle her out of her daze.

No response.

"Ma'am?" I tried a little louder. With that, she seemed to blink awake.

"Oh, hello!" she said, standing up and stretching. Her words were a little sluggish and tired. "I'm Deborah. Glad to meet you!"

We introduced ourselves. And then we offered to buy her dinner. She was pretty shocked, but she happily accepted. "That would be incredible," she said. "Can't remember the last time I ate anything."

What happened next? Well, we walked with our new acquaintance to a sandwich shop, bought her an egg salad sandwich and some hot tea, and shared a little conversation.

"You both have changed my entire day," she said when her meal arrived. "This looks so good."

We were really late by this time, so Dave and I ducked out of the coffee shop and began running toward the restaurant where the others were waiting for us. We ran in silence, but the whole way there, I was thinking: *A simple decision to take a few minutes out of my busy day and a few dollars out of my pocket had helped out a person in need and completely changed her day.*

Jesus boiled his story down to one profound question: "Which of these three was a neighbor to this man?"

Sometimes the answer is so simple: Loving your neighbor requires making a decision to be neighborly.

Question

Identify a person (or group of people) your life touches who you tend to stay away from, or who you're happy someone else is responsible for. Then ask yourself what you can do to be a neighbor...and if you are willing to do it.

Fact

Median monthly income for a homeless person is half the federal poverty level.

> *Jesus, thank You for treating me like a neighbor, even though sometimes I don't deserve it. You don't ever pass me by when I'm hurt. You heal me and take care of me. Help me to love my neighbors in the same way. And help me to remember that my neighbor is anyone who needs my help. Absolutely anyone. Amen.*

2.7

ACTION DAY #2

*The only thing necessary for the triumph
of evil is for good men to do nothing.*
EDMUND BURKE

hope and pray that you had a great experience during last week's Action Day. What kind of results or personal insights can you trace to those activities? Make sure you take the time to record today's experiences and your changes in the "Notes to Self" sections.

Now it's time for the second Action Day of your *Under the Overpass* experience.

OPTION 1: CONSOLE GIFT CERTIFICATES

A concern most of us have about being generous to the homeless is that they'll use our money for drugs or alcohol.

I wish that I could tell you differently, but Sam and I saw a lot of the money given to panhandlers go straight to drugs or alcohol. Still, these men and women are human beings, and human beings need to eat. So the challenge is to meet needs without feeding addictions.

Here's an idea:

Go to a coffee shop or a fast food restaurant and purchase gift certificates for an amount somewhere between $5 and $10. Put these in the console of your car or in your purse or briefcase, and the next time you see someone in need, you can offer a certificate. Doing so provides a meal or a cup of coffee, but no alcohol or drugs.

OPTION 2: VOLUNTEER AT A LOCAL RESCUE MISSION

Rescue missions exist in every major metropolitan area across the United States. These are incredible organizations that offer services for the local homeless. For example, men and women can come in for a warm meal, perhaps get some clothing, receive encouragement and friendship, and maybe sleep for the night. But one of the biggest struggles for missions is in the numbers—a tiny staff serving scores or even hundreds of people every day.

Do the math. How is a needy person going to get meaningful time with a caring person?

You can be part of a solution. Go to www.agrm.org and find the mission closest to you. Call them up to ask if there's any opportunity for you to come down and volunteer some time. You'll definitely get stretched out of your comfort zone, but you won't have to do anything you don't already know how to do. You might be asked to organize the clothing donations or serve at mealtime or simply visit with lonely, forgotten people over dinner. Missions with rehabilitation programs offer more long-term possibilities. For example, the men and women in these programs need mentors to help guide them through their recovery. Even if you're not a trained counselor, one hour a week spent with a person who's trying to build a new life can make a huge impact.

OPTION 3: SPAGHETTI DINNER FOR THE HOMELESS

I'm a huge fan of spaghetti. It's easy to make, nutritious, filling, and tastes awesome. Lots of street people feel the same. It's even easy to chew for those without teeth! So my wife and I occasionally take spaghetti dinners to the homeless in our hometown. It's a ton of fun to do, especially with friends. Here's how to serve dinner to about fifteen (very surprised) people. At a grocery store, buy:

> 2 big packets of dried spaghetti noodles
> 1 industrial-sized can of tomato sauce
> some fresh olives, garlic, and tomatoes
> 2 loaves of fresh French bread
> Parmesan cheese
> 15 take-out boxes
> plastic forks
> paper napkins

Head home and make all of the spaghetti up. Then, fill the take-out boxes with heaping helpings of spaghetti and a slice or two of warm French bread. Stack them five to a paper bag with handles (to make your walking easier). Then head downtown, park, and walk around the sidewalks, offering a plate of "homemade spaghetti with fresh bread" to the men and women you encounter. Watch their eyes light up with amazement as you ask them if they'd like some Parmesan cheese on their steaming spaghetti!

Most of this week's actions require you to be a little more willing to engage with people who most of us wouldn't otherwise connect with. You'll probably feel hesitant and a little intimidated. If you do, I completely understand. It's normal to be afraid of the unfamiliar. Pray the prayer of commitment below, and ask the Lord to give you the boldness necessary to reach out for His kingdom.

Fact

There are about three hundred rescue missions across the country.

> *Lord God, thank You for preparing me to do work for You. Honestly, I'm a little bit uncertain about what I'm stepping into. I know that You're going to be there with me every step of the way, but I'm still nervous. Would You help me to have the courage and the boldness to reach out and really make a difference in the lives of these needy people? Amen.*

NOTES TO SELF

a. Something God showed me this week:

b. A question I've pondered this week:

c. Someone I met this week I want to remember:

d. A decision I've made this week to change how I live:

e. More notes to self:

WEEK
THREE

3.1

ROOM IN THE INN

"We have only five loaves here and two fish...."
And they all ate and were satisfied....
And those who ate were about five
thousand men, besides women and children.

MATTHEW 14:17, 20–21

hen it comes to the overwhelming needs around us, you have to ask the question: Can one person make a difference?

My answer is, "Yes...but."

Yes, first of all, because look at how a few people and their sack lunch fed thousands when Jesus entered the equation. Can the same Savior change a life, meet a need, and make history through a no-namer like you or me? Absolutely. In fact, I think God likes doing that sort of thing again and again so we can't help but marvel at the miracles that happen all around us.

And now for the "...but." One person can make a difference in our world, but...that one person will make an even bigger difference when they decide to help mobilize others. Then, impossible things become *even more* possible.

I know. I've seen it happen. Remember the college students in Santa Barbara who feed thirty or forty homeless men and women every week? They hardly have a budget. There's no building, no legal structure, no federal grant, no press release. It's just a band of students who've decided to do something together they could never do apart. And think of the impact on the hungry and the homeless in America if, say, one in every ten churches or one in every ten colleges or one in every ten high schools decided to do something similar.

Guess what—it's starting to happen. One idea I'm aware of is called Room in the Inn, a plan to serve the homeless in an area by bringing together local churches to do the work. The idea was created in Nashville and has spread from there.

Here's how it works: Seven churches band together to open their sanctuaries to the homeless and hungry in their area during winter months. Each church is responsible for one night per week. On its assigned night, the church takes a bus downtown and gathers twenty or so homeless people who are willing to try out the church's hospitality. The bus brings the guests back to the church, where other members of the ministry have prepared a gourmet meal. People from the church join the guests for food and conversation. After dinner it's off for a hot shower (if the church has the facilities). Then clean medical scrubs get handed out (for pajamas), and the guests settle in for a good night's sleep in a warm, safe environment. Meanwhile, their clothes go to the homes of other church members for cleaning, repairing, and replacing, if necessary. By morning the clothes are back and ready for use—just in time for the guests to enjoy a hot breakfast. Before they're taken back to more familiar surroundings, each visitor gets a sack lunch.

Next night, it's another church's responsibility. And so it goes until the next week rolls around and the cycle repeats.

You can imagine some of the practical problems: dealing with shocked church folk, for example, when a dirty sock is discovered in the sanctuary on Sunday. Or trying to serve inebriated or mentally impaired visitors in an orderly yet loving manner. But you gotta love the vision, the courage, the resourcefulness, the humility...the results.

The thing is, none of us can take lightly God's concern for the poor and His commandments to love others. There's no room for that in the Bible, and there's too much need all around us.

Here's a crazy statement, but I believe it's true: Wherever you are, an amazing adventure of faith is just waiting for you, as well as a crew of friends who want to join you. Maybe you don't feel like you have anything to bring to the table except for a few slimy fish and some moldy bread.

But just trust Him.

Miracles are miraculous because everybody thought what happened was impossible.

Be willing to step out, put it in Christ's hands, and see what happens next.

Question

Stop and think for a few moments. What might God have given you that He wants to use to impact someone else today? (Remember the loaves and fish.) Maybe it's your lunch money, the car you drive, or your basketball shoes. Are you willing to let God use them?

*If a man cannot be a Christian where he is,
he cannot be a Christian anywhere.*

HENRY WARD BEECHER

*Lord, help me to see through Your eyes the things that
You've given me. Help me to understand that when
I give what I have to You, You can use it in tremen-
dous ways to impact lots of lives. Remove my fear of
being laughed at, my fear of being inadequate, my
fear of being ineffective, so You can work through me.
Everything is Yours, Lord. Help me to live that way.
Amen.*

A MIGHTY LOAF

*Jesus looked up and saw the rich putting their gifts
into the offering box, and he saw a poor widow put in
two small copper coins. And he said, "Truly, I tell you,
this poor widow has put in more than all of them.
For they all contributed out of their abundance, but she
out of her poverty put in all she had to live on."*

LUKE 21:1–4

t's easy today to live by really bad math. We think our
worth is all about how much expensive stuff we have.
And we think the gift gets better the more zeros there
are on the check. By that math, the CEO who gives a million dollars is more generous than the high school student
who gives his sweatshirt to a shivering homeless man on a
cold night.

God's math is different. Really different. Read the

verses from Luke again. "More," according to Jesus, has to do with *what's left* after you give, not just *how much* you gave.

Late one night in Portland, Sam and I were sitting outside of a long-closed coffee shop on chairs that were chained to the table, which was bolted into the cement. Chilly air blew off the Willamette River, but we were peacefully journaling while we munched on a piece of discarded pizza we'd found earlier.

After about a half hour, a homeless guy named Ron walked by.

Ron was about fifty years old, deeply tanned and wrinkled. The white stubble on his chin made his weathered face look even darker. He wore a beat-up hat and a torn, gray wool coat.

He told us he was headed to a large homeless camp under a nearby interstate bridge for the night.

After about ten minutes of conversation, Ron invited us to come to the camp if we needed a place to sleep. We thanked him but pointed to a nearby marina, our favorite sleeping spot.

"Police don't bother you there?" Ron asked, eyebrows

raised in concern. "Had a buddy not too long ago spent time in jail 'cause he slept there. Be careful!"

With that, he walked away, and Sam and I went back to writing. But a couple of minutes later, Ron was back and pulling a round loaf of wheat bread out of his coat pocket.

"Hey, you guys hungry, by chance?" he asked. "I just picked this up from a bakery down that ways." He motioned down the riverfront. "Honestly, I ain't gonna eat this whole thing."

Sam and I glanced at one another in surprise, then turned back to Ron. We had shared one piece of vegetarian pizza for dinner and were still quite hungry.

"You sure?" Sam asked, wanting to make sure we weren't taking Ron's dinner.

"Yeah. Why hold on to it? Somehow I always find food! Don't worry about tomorrow, it will take care of itself, someone once said."

"I think it was Jesus," I said, smiling.

Ron smiled. "Smart man, that Jesus was. Son of God, you know."

"That He is," Sam said. "We're both Christians."

"Well, all the more then, brothers!" Ron's face lit up in a huge smile. "Seriously, take the rest of this thing." And with that he gripped the loaf, tore it in half, and gave us the larger piece.

With a final "Enjoy!" Ron walked away, seemingly happy for the opportunity to give his dinner to a couple of other homeless guys.

Sam and I were blown away.

"He just gave us more than half of what he found for dinner tonight," Sam said.

"Yeah," I said, thinking. "You ever given half of your dinner to someone else?"

"Nope."

"Me neither."

We have a lot to learn about generosity from those in poverty. Mother Teresa said, "It's not how much you give but how much love you put into the giving." If we're talking about giving out of love, love demands sacrifice.

Question

What is one thing you can sacrifice today in order to bless someone else? Don't let anything stop you from doing it.

If our charities do not at all pinch or hamper us,
I should say they are too small.

C. S. LEWIS, *MERE CHRISTIANITY*

Lord, thank You that You don't look at our bank
accounts to determine our worth. Help me to live that
way too, and not be so caught up in stuff and money.
Let the story of the widow who gave two pennies and
the homeless man who gave half his dinner push me to
be generous in new ways. Help me to sacrifice so that
I can love others and help make a difference. Amen.

FRINGE EMBRACE

A new commandment I give to you,
that you love one another: just as I have loved you,
you also are to love one another.
By this all people will know that you are my disciples,
if you have love for one another.

JOHN 13:34–35

t was month four of our five-month journey. The lower desert in Phoenix, Arizona, even in October, is hot enough by day to fry you and cool enough by night to give you the chills. After three weeks bumming around the downtown, trying to escape the heat in the library, Sam and I decided to take a bus out to the nearby city of Scottsdale. "It's not as rough out there," a homeless guy named Carl had told us.

There we were, riding through the desert twilight on a bus. We were tired, hungry, thirsty, and anxious for our road trip/adventure in faith to end. Next to me, Sam leaned against a window, head dropped down in sleep. One more city to go—San Diego—then we'd be done. We couldn't wait.

At the next stop, a guy who looked about twenty sat down across the aisle from me with his headphones on, volume cranked high enough for me to hear. It was a popular Christian worship band—my favorite. The guy stared out the opposite window, mouthing the lyrics, never acknowledging my presence.

Then he pulled out a bag of barbecue potato chips— my favorite—and began munching away. My stomach growled loudly. Good thing his music was so loud or he might have heard it. The title track came on: "Teach me to love others in Your name, Lord."

With every passing mile I was growing more cynical. It was just about all I could do to not reach across the aisle, pull his worship-music-blaring headphones off his ears, and ask for some chips.

When he got off at a stop, I was almost relieved.

When we got to Scottsdale, the night air felt suddenly cool. We pulled on dirty sweatshirts and decided to hike back about a mile to a huge church campus we'd noticed, hoping to find a spot for the night. Sam and I walked in silence, both of us feeling exhaustion deep in our souls.

At the church, we found a spot in the shadows at the back of the sanctuary, away from the street lights and traffic, and curled up in our bags.

Next thing I knew, I awakened with a start to bright sunlight and a voice.

"Can I help you guys?" said the voice. I struggled to find my glasses.

"Uh," I said, still unsure of where I was. "Where am I?"

"Next to our church. Can I help you?"

"Um..." Sam was awake now too, and stretching. "What time is it?" We were stalling, both of us expecting to get escorted politely back to the sidewalk.

"Six thirty," the man said. "You guys wait here while you wake up. I'll be back."

Huh. This guy was actually half-nice.

Sam and I packed up and moved to a nearby picnic table to warm up in the morning sun. Before long, the church guy had returned, carrying something that nearly brought tears to my eyes.

"Coffee?" he asked.

"Didn't know if you would want cream and sugar, but I brought some just in case."

He set the coffee down in front of us, then plates with two toasted bagels and cream cheese for both of us.

I wanted to jump up and hug the guy I was so excited, but I figured my stench would send him reeling, so I held back. Sam and I were both trying to stammer out our thanks when he broke in.

"Oh, and we have some showers in the back you can use to clean up when you've finished breakfast. Just knock on this door here, and we'll show you where they're at."

Later, freshly showered and hugely encouraged, we tried again to thank our host. But he wouldn't hear any of it.

"C'mon. This is a church. It's what we do. If you need anything else, you know where to come."

By now the desert was heating up again, heading for another ninety-plus-degree day. Walking back to catch our bus, I heard those lyrics again in my head: "Teach me to love others in Your name." This morning, though, they sounded different—real, honest, and full of hope.

Question

What does "loving one another" really look like in your life? Do you love others in a way that shows people you're a follower of Christ? What are some tangible ways you can love others in this way today?

> *Jesus, please help me to be aware of the needs around me and not be so distracted that I miss out on ways to help people. Make me willing to use what I have, what You've given me, to bless someone else. Help me be open to that today, and when all of the reasons why I shouldn't offer what I have start running through my head, give me the courage to continue forward. Open my eyes, Lord, and let me see the situation as You see it! Amen.*

GOLDEN GATE JAM SESSION

We love because he first loved us.

1 JOHN 4:19

W e arrived back at the mouth of San Francisco's Golden Gate Park after dark with three cold ninety-nine-cent burgers to show for a day's worth of strumming and singing downtown. Fog had rolled in off the Pacific by then and cast the park in a soft, dream-like light.

At the end of Haight Street, Sam and I slung off our backpacks and guitars near a large planter, nodding hellos to the people who were there and looking for familiar faces. A guy named "Y," whom we had met earlier in the week, quickly came up with a plan for us.

"Guys, you know what I think?" he said excitedly. "I think you should bust out your guitars again tonight."

We didn't feel too enthusiastic somehow, but we agreed anyway. "Grab your conga!" Sam said, and Y ran off into the park to retrieve his instrument. In the meantime, Sam and I settled down to dinner.

We'd each finished one burger, and I had just pulled out burger number three to split when Y returned, his conga hanging from his back with a makeshift strap.

"You guys gonna eat that?" Y asked hungrily, pointing to the rest of our dinner.

Sam and I looked at each other. Actually, we were pretty amazed Y wanted to eat a fast-food burger. A lot of people we met in San Francisco refused to eat from burger joints. An interesting twist to the homeless experience in this town: vegetarian lifestyles.

"Hey, why don't you take it?" Sam said.

When Y finished eating, Sam and I pulled out our guitars and began playing together. I played rhythm, and Sam picked out a great lead riff. Y began pounding on his conga, and a great melody unfolded. It was incredible to see the mood of the music carry itself along.

Soon people shuffled over from other parts of the park. A few other musicians appeared as well, including an older guy named Rock who had displayed incredible guitar skills during a previous jam session. Once we finished our song, I let out a cheer and handed my guitar to Rock.

The music got even better, and a whole lot louder, as Rock covered songs from the sixties, seventies, and eighties. More and more musicians arrived. Another conga arrived, as did a tambourine. People sang along, song blended into song, and time slipped away.

Suddenly, a collective cheer went up midsong, and the music abruptly stopped. Sam and I looked around, unsure of what was gong on. Then we realized that a line was forming, leading down the street to a folding table, where a small group of twentysomethings was busy setting out dinner—baskets of rolls, salad containers, jugs of orange juice, and a huge stainless-steel pot full of soup.

Sam and I grabbed our packs and headed for the end of the line. When our turn came, we filled up our plates with an incredible meal. At the end of the food line, we read a sign:

Jesus loves all. We're trying to. Can we help?

We talked to the three guys and three girls behind the table for a while. They were from a local Christian group home that allowed people traveling between different permanent housing situations to live in the building indefinitely in exchange for a small rent and community service.

Good idea.

The sign hanging off of their table said something that hit me pretty hard. I thought of 1 John 4:19: "We love because he first loved us." The strongest motivation for loving others is a true understanding of God's love for us, because when we're honest with ourselves, we really aren't very lovable.

Despite all our junk, God has accepted us in Christ.

And He's commanded us to love others in exactly the same way.

Question

Does Christ's love for you motivate your actions toward others? What are some tangible ways that you love others because God first loved you?

> *Be faithful in the little practices of love,*
> *which will build in you the life of holiness*
> *and make you Christ-like.*
> MOTHER TERESA

Jesus, thank You for accepting me, even though I carry so much stuff with me. Help me to realize more about how incredible Your love for me really is. Let my attitude toward others be affected by my amazement at Your love. Remind me constantly today, for there will be lots to distract me. Gently put Your love on my mind again and again, and show me how I can better respond to the people right in front of me because of Your love. Amen.

MINISTRY OF INTERRUPTIONS

He had an only daughter, about twelve years of age, and she was dying. As Jesus went, the people pressed around him. And there was a woman who had had a discharge of blood for twelve years, and though she had spent all of her living on physicians, she could not be healed by anyone. She came up behind him and touched the fringe of his garment, and immediately her discharge of blood ceased. And Jesus said, "Who was it that touched me?" When all denied it, Peter said, "Master, the crowds surround you and are pressing in on you!" But Jesus said, "Someone touched me, for I perceive that power has gone out from me." And when the woman saw that she was not hidden, she came trembling, and falling down before him declared in the presence of all the people why she had touched him, and how she had been immediately healed. And he said to her, "Daughter, your faith has made you well; go in peace."

LUKE 8:42–48

don't know about you, but I've gotten pretty good at lining up the different roles I have to play every day, then running through them as efficiently as possible.

Your list might look different, but here's mine for a typical day:

1. Follower of Christ
2. Husband in progress
3. Developing tea connoisseur
4. Aspiring computer programmer
5. Writer and speaker
6. Road-rage driver in a rush
7. Friend, slow at responding to e-mail
8. Occasional son on cell phone
9. Weirdo talking to street person

Makes you wonder, though. What happens when the roles collide? Like when "road-rage driver" slams into "follower of Christ." Talk about embarrassing and inconvenient! Most of us hope the different "compartments" of our lives stay as separate as possible. It's embarrassing and frustrating when they collide because often they're completely at odds.

Our Christian life doesn't (or shouldn't) work like that, though. We shouldn't be more spiritual during our "quiet time" in the morning or our prayer before we fall asleep than when we're dealing with the checkout clerk at the supermarket. That's why Paul says, "Whatever you do, in word or deed, do everything in the name of the Lord Jesus" (Colossians 3:17). Our faith in Christ ought to influence every moment of all our days, rather than just one day per week, or only during times of "ministry."

Look at Jesus' example in today's reading. These verses come in the middle of one of the busiest chapters in the Bible. Jesus' list of roles for these couple of days included:

1. Traveling evangelist (on foot, mind you)
2. Spiritual healer
3. Storyteller
4. Teacher
5. Son and brother
6. Sailor
7. Mentor to His disciples
8. Weather controller (bad storm on the lake)
9. Physician

But while the disciples and the crowds are constantly pushing Him to hurry to the next thing, Jesus stops to ask a simple question: "Who was it that touched Me?"

I'll paraphrase where it went from there.

Disciples, cranky and impatient: "Jesus, come on!

Everyone is touching you. Now, let's get a move on! We've got another miracle to perform with this guy's daughter!"

Jesus, quietly: "No, a person touched my cloak."

Then he waited until the woman came forward and told Him what she needed from Him.

His response: "Daughter, your faith has made you well."

This story reminds us that whatever task Jesus was involved in, He was *always* at work doing His Father's business (see John 5:17).

I have a friend who often says that Jesus led a "ministry of interruptions." What he means is that Jesus didn't mind being interrupted. *People* interrupted Him, and *people* were the reason He came in the first place.

Of course, the same applies to you and me today. We're commanded to love others, yet so often we view others as interruptions or inconveniences because they don't fit into the compartment of our lives we're focused on at that moment.

This point was brought home to me by a funny experience during our travels. (Actually, it wasn't funny to begin with.)

We found a place to sleep next to the sanctuary of another large church in Phoenix. The next morning we awoke to a wondrous scene—trays and trays of steaming breakfast being carried into a building across the church campus. The delicious aroma of pancakes, eggs, and sausages made us think we'd slept our way into heaven.

Well, not really. The breakfast, you see, wasn't for us. Within a few minutes of being spotted, we were firmly escorted off the church property by a neatly dressed church member. I don't have to tell you how let down, disappointed, and, yes, starving Sam and I felt as we walked away.

But that's not the end of the story. The next morning Sam and I decided to return to that very church for their Sunday-morning service.

All went as you'd expect until the end of the service. Just as we were about to leave, we heard a yell from the back of the sanctuary: "Guys, guys, guys!"

We turned to see a man running across the back of the church, down the main aisle, and right up to us, where he threw his arms around us. And get this—it was the man who twenty-four hours earlier had kicked us off the church grounds!

"Guys!" the man blurted. Tears began to well up in his eyes. "Guys, I'm so sorry. And I'm so glad you came back. Forgive me. I can't believe I did that. I'm so sorry. We were having a church breakfast, and I kicked you out of the church when I should have invited you in. Really, I'm sorry." The tears were flowing now.

Wow, I thought, trying to find words. "Well, that's okay. We forgive you. See, we're almost used to it by now."

"But that's just it!" the man said. "Christians should never make you accustomed to rejection. If there is anywhere you should be accepted and loved, it should be at a church."

Then the man turned more embarrassed than tearful. "You want to know something funny? I'm a director of homeless outreach in this area."

Silence. Then we all burst out laughing. I think God did too. Before long, we'd made a new friend.

In today's world, keeping our faith life in convenient little boxes is a common problem. Most of us have so much stuff going on that the only way we can survive is to compartmentalize. For this guy, homeless ministry was on Tuesday evenings, not Saturday mornings when he was helping set up for the breakfast! On Saturday morning, Sam and I weren't people in need. We were simply a very inconvenient (and smelly) interruption.

Question

How many people will you interact with today? Five? Ten? Maybe even a hundred? There are countless opportunities for God to work through us to impact other people, if we're willing to let Him interrupt us with needs. What are some ways you can "decompartmentalize" so that God can use you today to bless others?

> *Lord, I don't want to compartmentalize my faith.*
> *I want it to be in every part of my day. So, when I*
> *get too distracted to think of You, interrupt me!*
> *Shockingly, if You must, so that I can live for You and*
> *not be hypocritical. Maybe there's a lot of change*
> *necessary in me. I want to change, Father! Amen.*

LOVING JESUS. REALLY.

Is such the fast that I choose, a day for a person to humble himself?... Will you call this a fast, and a day acceptable to the Lord? Is not this the fast that I choose: to loose the bonds of wickedness, to undo the straps of the yoke, to let the oppressed go free, and to break every yoke? Is it not to share your bread with the hungry and bring the homeless poor into your house; when you see the naked, to cover him, and not to hide yourself from your own flesh?

ISAIAH 58:5-7

L
ate one evening in DC, Sam and I sat on a street corner panhandling as the pedestrian traffic started to die down. When the streets were empty, we gave up trying to raise more money and just started having fun with our guitars. In the middle of our rendition of the fast-paced Jars of Clay song "Flood," a group of teenagers

came walking down the street. As they neared us, one guy's face lit up with pleasant surprise.

"Hey, that song is by Jars of Clay!" he said, jabbing one of his friends in the ribs.

Sam and I looked up. "Yeah, it is! You know Jars?"

"Sure," the guy said. He and his friends stopped for a while to sing along as we ended the song. We went straight into another Jars song, this one a little slower and more of a typical worship song. Late that night on a deserted downtown street, the strums and voices rose into the night sky, and five complete strangers were united in worship.

About midway through our time in the next city, Portland, I woke up before sunrise. You know how sometimes you're just awake and your mind is alive? I looked up to a nearby bridge and wondered what the sunrise would look like from its high vantage points. I scrawled a note to Sam in case he woke up while I was gone, grabbed my Bible and journal, and set out.

I reached one of the high spots on the bridge in about ten minutes and scrambled to a perilous but picturesque perch. From my spot, I was looking down on both the predawn city shimmering in the wind and toward the warm blue glow in the east, growing brighter with every moment.

I broke open my Bible and poured over passage after passage in the pale light. I bounced from a psalm to a proverb to one of Paul's letters to Matthew. Maybe it was the height of my view or the rising sun covering the land with its light or just the joy of waking up to another day, but everything felt right that morning, and everything in me, around me, and coming out of me, was worship.

In a conversation not too long ago, I was told of a shocking situation. The man standing before me had been visiting an East Coast city on a recent trip. On Sunday he went to a local church to join their worship service. As he walked out of the service, he struck up a conversation with a woman who appeared homeless but also carried a small baby in her arms. While talking to her, he learned that she had been homeless, living in a cardboard box behind the church, for nearly two years. Her newly born daughter had spent more days outside than inside.

What's wrong with this picture? How does a church let a homeless mother and infant live in a box in the alley behind the church without notice for two years?

We're missing something as Christians if service is not a part of our lives. That's because worship requires service. Serving God and serving others. We simply can't forget that. Worship songs and quiet times, if we understand them, are meant to draw us closer to the heart of God, and that should always overflow into our lifestyles. There's so much more God is inviting us into than just singing or just thinking to ourselves how wonderful His creation is. God deeply desires for us to live out loud *because* of what we sing and think and pray. Jesus did spend time in the temple, He did spend time alone with the Father, but that's what enabled Him to *do* what the Father wanted.

Question

Are you spending time with God in prayer and song? Is that time leading you to serve people in the world around you? Spend some serious time with God and ask him to help you brainstorm ways to make service a part of your life. Then get out there and serve!

Fact

In this next year, about 1.35 million American children will experience homelessness.

Lord, thank You for the many ways You want us to worship You. I want to worship You in everything I do, from singing to writing to sports. Thank You for being such a creative God and giving us all of these things. But also help me to see and understand that service should be an integral part of my life too. I want to worship You by helping others. How do You want to use me? Show me, Lord! I will go! Amen.

ACTION DAY #3

So you also, when you have done
all that you were commanded, say,
"We are unworthy servants;
we have only done what was our duty."

LUKE 17:10

orship isn't just for Sunday mornings, as I'm sure
you've figured out by now. On this Action Day,
really focus on learning to see how serving others is
a form of worship. Nothing glorifies God more than sharing His love with others.

OPTION 1: VOLUNTEER AT A FOOD BANK

Food banks are organizations that collect household goods,
canned foods, and bare essentials for the needy. Your town
probably has one or more. Because they're largely volunteer-

run, food banks are a perfect opportunity to get involved. Give your local food bank a call and ask how you can help. They may ask you to help collect, organize, or deliver food. Take some friends along and be open to do whatever needs doing.

OPTION 2: MOTEL ROOM FOR A HOMELESS PERSON

Look outside your window right now. Maybe it's raining cats and dogs—but you, on the other hand, are dry. Maybe it's winter and a blizzard is raging outside—but you're warm as toast. Or, maybe it's ninety degrees out there—but, oh well, you're in an air-conditioned room. Think of this, though—homeless people are out there right now. They're not looking out the window at the weather; they're *living in it*. All day. All night. Which leads to this idea: Grab some friends, go downtown, and find a person who looks particularly uncomfortable with today's weather. Offer to purchase that person a meal and a night's stay at a motel.

OPTION 3: PANCAKE BREAKFAST FOR THE HOMELESS

Almost anyone can make and serve a great breakfast. Today, why don't you and a few friends make someone's day with a delicious spread? All you need is pancake mix and the simple ingredients required (read the label), syrup, butter, bacon or sausage, coffee (along with a big pot to brew it in), and utensils. Buy for a target number of "customers" (starting small is okay). Make the breakfast and brew the coffee; put the food, cups, plates, serving/eating utensils, and pot of coffee in the back of your car; and go looking for street people who might be hungry. Offer your free meal. You won't believe the surprised looks, the smiles, and the hearty appetites! I can't even begin to tell you what such a buffet would have done for Sam and me when we were on the streets. Waking up on concrete day after day is so draining, but to be met by genuine people offering a hot, homemade breakfast...well, that's a way to make someone feel loved!

God, thank You for all the things that I take for granted: my warm bed, my breakfast this morning, even every breath I take. I know that so many people in this world don't enjoy the same blessings. I'm so glad that You care for the poor and needy. Would You put that same love and compassion in my heart? I admit that sometimes it's so easy to just live as though these people don't even exist. But I want generosity to become a habit and a lifestyle for me. Continue to give me opportunities to make a difference and help me to take advantage of them. Amen.

NOTES TO SELF

[REFLECTIONS ON WEEK THREE]

a. Something God showed me this week:

_____

_____

_____

_____

_____

_____

_____

b. A question I've pondered this week:

_____

_____

_____

_____

_____

_____

_____

_____

c. Someone I met this week I want to remember:

d. A decision I've made this week to change how I live:

e. More notes to self:

WEEK
FOUR

HANDS AND FEET

Outdo one another in showing honor.

ROMANS 12:10

I awoke to a white and foggy world—San Francisco was living up to its reputation. It had been a long night on the concrete, and I hated the idea of stepping out of my warm bag into the cold. So I lay there watching dimly outlined figures walking past on the street.

Watching, that is, until I noticed that the homeless people going past were all definitely walking somewhere, and with definite purpose. So I heaved myself out of the bag to inquire.

"What's going on, man?" I asked the next guy in dreads to go by.

"Pancake breakfast at a church, bro!" he said, his smile revealing rotten teeth.

"Awesome!" I exclaimed, and turned to wake up Sam.

We hastily packed up and joined the exodus.

About a mile down the road we saw the Promised Land, a warehouselike church with men and women streaming in through the front doors.

Inside, we encountered an incredible sight: more than a hundred ragged people sitting down around tables heaping with food and about twenty or so less ragged men, women, and teenagers bustling about, taking empty plates, bringing more food, or refilling cups of orange juice and coffee.

What struck me most, though, was not what they were doing, but how they were doing it. You wouldn't find better service at a country club. Their every step expressed a genuine desire to serve and respect, to affirm and encourage their filthy guests of honor.

As I stood there gaping, two volunteers stepped up and offered to take my backpack and guitar in exchange for a claim number. When I nodded, they assured me that my gear would be safe until I picked it up after the meal. When they helped me take off my crusty pack, they exercised the kind of care most would reserve for handling expensive china.

A clean-cut, responsible-looking man of about forty

noticed my overwhelmed expression, smiled, and nodded toward the food line. "Right that way, sir. Enjoy!"

And enjoy we did! As we were waiting in line for our plates, a new song came over the sound system. "Audio Adrenaline?" Sam asked.

"Yep. 'Hands and Feet.'"

A lady behind the counter looked up and smiled at us as we held our plates. "One sausage link or two?" she asked.

"Two please," Sam and I said at the same time, cherishing the respect and dignity we felt in getting to make that simple choice.

> Wanna be your hands,
> Wanna be your feet.
> I'll go where you send me,
> Go where you send me.

All the way down that mouth-watering breakfast line, I listened to those lyrics.

I wondered what it was like for these men and women to wake up early on a Saturday morning, come to their church, make a pancake breakfast, and be welcoming, kind, and loving toward any vagrant who walked through the door. Probably not very easy.

I wondered too about the Son of God, stretched out on the cross.

It was His hands and His feet that held Him to the cross.

That's not very easy either.

Love is most clearly seen through sacrifice. Being the hands and feet of Christ means it's our responsibility to communicate God's love for people through our genuine acts of service, even when it's hard.

Paul exhorted early Christians to "outdo one another in showing honor." You know what showing honor looks like? I do. It looks like a free pancake breakfast out of nowhere on a foggy morning served with genuine concern, compassion, and respect to a room full of stinky homeless people no one really cares about.

That's being the hands and feet of Christ.

Question

How could you "outdo someone in showing honor" today? Think about ways to bless someone who would really be surprised by your willingness to do something out of the ordinary.

> *We want a fiercer delight*
> *and a fiercer discontent.*
> G. K. CHESTERTON, *ORTHODOXY*

Lord, I want to truly love people, and I'm so thankful that You have created so many ways to do that. I want to show people that they are valuable in Your eyes, Father. Please show me who You want me to reach out to today and help me to not be afraid to do it. I want what I do to bring You glory and help other people know You better. Amen.

TRUE FEAST

> *[Jesus] said also to the man who had invited him,*
> *"When you give a dinner or a banquet, do not invite your*
> *friends or your brothers or your relatives or rich neighbors,*
> *lest they also invite you in return and you be repaid.*
> *But when you give a feast, invite the poor, the crippled, the*
> *lame, the blind, and you will be blessed, because they cannot*
> *repay you. You will be repaid at the resurrection of the just."*
>
> LUKE 14:12–14

When throwing a party, for eternal reward, you need a guest list full of the least likely people you can imagine, people who can never pay you back, never make you feel cool for inviting them. Sounds crazy, huh? Jesus' way of doing things was often hard to accept.

One night in Phoenix on our way to a sleeping spot we liked, Sam and I passed a five-star hotel with well-dressed people milling about in front of the entrance and luxury sedans pulling up to drop off more partygoers.

Sam and I walked across the red carpet at the entrance, trying our best to be invisible (it didn't work). Then we stopped to look through the window into a beautifully decorated ballroom packed full of people. Toward the front of the room a large sign read, "Happy Birthday!" Waiters dressed in white tuxedos passed through the crowd carrying silver platters heaped with expensive-looking appetizers.

We stared silently, separated from another world only by a window.

A waiter passed by with a full platter of baked chicken dripping with rich sauce.

"Sam," I said, only half-joking, "I'll bet we could run in there, grab one of those trays, and be back outside, no problem."

Sam laughed. "Check out the security over there!" Two very large and intimidating guys were checking people's coats at the door. Any dreams of tender baked chicken evaporated.

We felt like kids pressing our noses against the candy display at an old-time country store. Everything we so badly wanted was just out of reach.

Just then an older gentleman right in front of us grabbed a glass of champagne from one of the waiters. He tilted his head back for a quick drink and noticed us standing outside looking in. With a warm smile he raised his glass toward us in salute.

Sam and I gave an embarrassed wave, nodded, and walked away.

"*That* was awkward," Sam said.

"Sure was," I said.

We walked away in silence. We needed to stop drooling, find our sleeping spot for the night, roll out our bags, and forget about birthdays, banquets, and chicken on a silver tray.

Just as I was about to drift to sleep, I reached for my Bible. I remembered reading about Jesus' party tips.

"Sam, dude, listen to this," I said, and began reading in Luke 14 where Jesus talks about how to throw a party of eternal proportions: "When you give a feast, invite the poor, the crippled, the lame, the blind, and you will be blessed, because they cannot repay you. You will be repaid at the resurrection of the just."

"Have you ever seen anything like that?" I asked when I was finished. "I mean, what would that kind of party look like today?"

"Dunno," said Sam. "I've never even been to a party with appetizers on a silver platter! But imagine—a whole ballroom filled with the weak, the drunk, the blind, the homeless. Let's do it!"

We both thought for a moment. The more we thought, the better the plan sounded.

"But maybe we shouldn't serve champagne," I said. We both laughed. We agreed that, instead of party favors, at our banquet we'd hand out groceries or new sleeping bags.

Just before we dropped off to sleep, Sam asked the obvious question: "Do you think anybody would be willing to do what it takes to throw a party like that?"

Probably not, we decided.

You have to ask, though: Why not? Why not throw a party Jesus' way? Why do thousands of Christians read this story every year *but never actually do it*?

Question

What would it be like to throw a feast for homeless people at a nice restaurant in your hometown? What generous deed could you do today for a person you *know* can never pay you back?

We either add to the darkness of indifference...
or we light a candle to see by.
MADELEINE L'ENGLE, *A CIRCLE OF QUIET*

Jesus, I'm so glad You said things that challenge me to be different. I love how You take the things of this world and turn them on their heads! Give me the boldness that I need to actually do what You say. Help me see all the possibilities! Amen.

HOMELESS FAMILY

Do nothing from rivalry or conceit, but in humility count others more significant than yourselves. Let each of you look not only to his own interests, but also to the interests of others.

PHILIPPIANS 2:3–4

Hiking uphill toward San Francisco's Golden Gate Park felt more like walking up Mt. Everest. We'd spent all afternoon sitting on the platform at a subway stop in downtown San Francisco, playing, singing, and hoping for spare change. We hadn't come up with much. Only enough for either a) two train passes to get back to the park for the night or b) two fast-food meals.

We chose fast food...and a long walk home.

My backpack felt like it weighed a good two hundred pounds, and frankly, I felt like pitching my guitar into the Pacific Ocean. It wasn't good for anything in this city, anyway. Why should I have to lug it around?

By the time we slung our packs off at the park an hour and a half later, all I wanted to do was just lie there and not move for a very, very long time. Sam and I stretched out to rest, even though it was early.

I was just beginning to doze off when I heard a baby laughing.

A baby laughing?

I opened my eyes and stared up into a dark night sky, and then the laughter came again. I sat up and looked around. Down the sidewalk, a family consisting of a mom, a dad, and a baby in a stroller had paused next to a group of homeless people. One of the homeless guys was making faces at the baby, who looked like she was really enjoying herself.

Just then, the father pulled three meals in Styrofoam containers out of a sack and handed them out. While he did that, the mom produced forks and napkins. After visiting with the men while they ate, the little family said good-bye and started walking in our direction.

When they arrived, they had huge smiles on their faces and immediately walked around the stroller to introduce themselves—Gina and Jose, each about thirty, and their beautiful eleven-month-old daughter.

"You guys hungry?" Jose asked, starting to reach into the same sack. "We've got spaghetti with meat balls, vegetables, and mashed potatoes. Really good stuff. We ate some ourselves about an hour ago."

This was incredible! Sam and I eagerly accepted their offer, and I'm pretty sure our eyes got just as big as the other homeless guys' did as we opened the boxes and saw the heaping portions inside. This food would last each of us two days!

"We're living at a church up the street a bit—" Jose motioned down Haight Street—"and this was our dinner this evening."

"How long have you been there?" Sam asked.

"Oh, about two weeks. We came up from Los Angeles. I couldn't get any work, and our cash ran out, so we were on the streets for a while."

"Then this church started helping us," Gina chimed in with a smile. "They let us live in their offices. They always serve dinner, and there's always extra food, so Jose and I thought we could share the extra food with people like us still on the streets."

Jose explained that they had started sharing their food after hearing a sermon on Philippians 2. "Do you guys have Bibles?" he asked. We both nodded. "Good. Philippians 2:3–4 says, 'Do nothing from rivalry or conceit, but in humility count others more significant than yourselves. Let each of you look not only to his own interests, but also to the interests of others.' We thought hard about how we could actually do what the Bible was saying we ought to do, and this is what we came up with."

Sam and I were amazed. Jose and Gina's willingness to put the Word of God into action had lifted our spirits, fed our bodies, and challenged us to see our own faith in a fresh light.

Believing you're a follower of Jesus who's called to put others (even strangers) first and look after their interests is not enough. Nothing changes, and Christ isn't honored, until something else happens.

You have to actually go and *do* it.

Question

How can you "count others more significant" than yourself? Think of at least one person you can put that Scripture into action with today.

> *Christ died for men precisely because men are*
> *not worth dying for: to make them worth it.*
> C. S. LEWIS, *THE WORLD'S LAST NIGHT*

Lord, thank You for literally loving me enough to die for me. You thought I was worth dying for, so You set the greatest example for me. Help me to put others first the way You do, to treat them like they are more important than me. Help me to serve others in a way that is really humble and unselfish. Amen!

PROSTITUTE LUCY

It is more blessed to give than to receive.

ACTS 20:35

I wish you could meet Lucy, a petite woman in her sixties with fire in her eyes and a whole city in her heart. I sat next to her a few weeks ago at a rescue mission fund-raising banquet in New Jersey. As we ate, she shared some of her story.

From the ages of sixteen to twenty-five, Lucy was a drug addict, an alcoholic, and a prostitute. She spent many of those years sharing a small apartment with several other prostitutes who sold themselves again and again to get money for drugs.

One day an older woman moved in to the same apartment building and took it upon herself to treat the prostitutes with the love of Jesus Christ. At first Lucy and her friends just laughed at the woman and her crazy religion. But as Lucy's lifestyle pulled her deeper into despair, the older woman's message began to have some impact.

"When I was twenty-five years old, the woman told me that Jesus Christ loved me and wanted more for me than a life of prostitution and drug addiction," Lucy said, her eyes filling up with tears. "And you know what? She was right. I gave my soul to Jesus, moved out of my apartment and into hers, and began getting cleaned up. I ain't never been the same since."

Every single one of Lucy's addictions literally disappeared the moment she accepted Christ. This obviously doesn't happen for everybody, but in Lucy's case, it did.

Within a year she had a job and had fallen in love with a good man. But when they married, she told him she knew where they were supposed to live—right back on the same street she used to walk looking for drugs and male customers. This time, though, she wanted to help the girls who were in the same place she once was.

And that's what she and her husband have been doing for the last forty years. "My door is always open," Lucy said, smiling. "Every one of those girls knows that if they need a safe place, they can come to Lucy's, and they'll never be turned away. Same with the homeless. Some winter nights we've had thirty people sleeping on our floors. Everyone knows if you need somethin', you come to Lucy's."

Toward the end of her story, Lucy looked intently at me and whispered, "You know what, Mike? I ain't never grown tired of this neither. Some people told me generosity can't last. Eventually you run out, they said. But they were wrong. After forty years, I'm filled up inside. When you help someone in the name of Jesus, His very power comes within you and fills you up the way drugs, alcohol, sex, money, nothin' can. That's why Jesus said, 'It's better to give than to receive.'"

Like I said, I sure wish you could meet Lucy.

Giving is a practice and a discipline. The more you do it, the easier it gets, and—as Lucy discovered—the more it fills you up.

Selfishness, on the other hand, is like cancer. Give it enough time, and it will eat you alive.

Question

Has someone ever been so kind and giving to you that you will never forget them? Think of something you can give to a person today that will affect their life for a long time.

*It is not a question of our equipment
but of our poverty, not of what we bring with us,
but of what God puts into us.*

OSWALD CHAMBERS, *MY UTMOST FOR HIS HIGHEST*

*Lord God in heaven, thank You for taking terrible
circumstances and turning them into amazing gifts.
I pray that You would teach me about the joy of self-
lessness and giving. Move my heart to be truly
generous with what You've given me. You can do so
much with so little, Father. How do You want to use
me, Lord? Open my heart and make me willing. Amen.*

WHO NEEDS A DOCTOR?

> *"Those who are well have no need of a physician,*
> *but those who are sick."*
>
> MATTHEW 9:12

Sam and I visited many churches where the members' disgust at our presence was obvious. One person literally stood in the foyer of a church with mouth agape as we walked past into the sanctuary. Sure, we were smelly and didn't look very clean or orderly. Our "Sunday best" was what we wore every day, the only clothes we had. But John the Baptist wore camel hair and ate locusts, and that sounds odder than our dirty, grubby attire!

Imagine this scene. You, sicker than can be, stumble into a doctor's office in search of something, anything, to help you get better. The receptionist glares at you as you approach the counter, looking as though he's going to be sick himself. When you ask for an appointment, you're rudely informed that *this* doctor's office simply doesn't allow sick people in the doors. You'll have to leave immediately. As you head out the door, you mutter to yourself something about where a sick person should go if not to the doctor.

This situation is both absurd and illogical. That's because, obviously, doctors exist to help sick people get better. Turning a person away from a doctor *because* they're sick is ludicrous.

Why should it be any different with the church? Jesus didn't come for the healthy, but for the sick. And when it comes to sin, the Bible paints a clear picture: We're *all* terminally ill. Does it make any sense, then, for us to ridicule or reject someone because their illness is more "visible" than our own? Instead, shouldn't we welcome them into a place where they can find a relationship with Christ, the only One who gives any of us hope?

We live in a world filled with people sorting through all sorts of junk. Some have problems with their families, some with their spouses, some with their siblings, some with their jobs, some with pornography, some with body image, some with greed, some with addiction, some with pride, some with jealousy. The list of human problems just goes on and on. What we proclaim as Christians is that Christ is the Way we must all go if we are to survive the illness that would otherwise destroy us.

When Sam and I walked into those churches where people just stared, frowned, or ignored us, they didn't know who we were. They didn't know that we already knew Christ or that, in a few months, we would be back into our normal lives, off the streets. For all they knew, this was the first time (and probably the last, based on how they treated us) that we had been to church.

The hardest part is that it isn't just "those people at the churches we went to" who do this. I do it. You do it. We all do. We all have access to the best Doctor (in Christ) possible, and so often we keep others from coming to Him because we don't think they fit in. What right do we have to keep people from knowing God? We are all in need of Christ, every single one of us. There is not one who is well on their own. In Christ alone we stand and live, are healed and are whole.

We must do all we can to look past what could be offensive in a person in order to welcome them into the body of Christ.

Question

Think of a person who may have felt turned away by the church because of their "sickness." What can you do to help undo those feelings of rejection and hurt?

> *The church is not a museum of*
> *saints but a hospital for sinners.*
> BRENNAN MANNING, *THE RAGAMUFFIN GOSPEL*

Lord, thank You for accepting me even though I'm sinful. Help me to never keep someone from knowing You because they don't fit my definition of a Christian. You can give the same new life to them that You gave to me. Help me to bring others closer to You, not push them away. Amen.

4.6

THE TALENTS

> *So then each of us will give*
> *an account of himself to God.*
> ROMANS 14:12

One of the most powerful movies I've ever seen is *Schindler's List*. Based on a true story, the Steven Spielberg film explores huge themes such as the corrupting influence of hatred and fear, the power of mercy, and the value of human life. More than anything, *Schindler's List* tells of the difference one life can make. (Just so you know, this R-rated movie is difficult to watch, extremely graphic, and not for everyone.)

Maybe you know the story. The setting is Europe during the 1940s, when Nazi forces are wreaking havoc across the continent. Oskar Schindler, a wealthy German businessman and member of the Nazi party, builds a successful business by manufacturing supplies for the troops in the war. Increasingly, he staffs his company with Jews he buys from Nazi prisons. Jews who don't make Schindler's hiring "list" are sure to be exterminated. By the end of the war, millions of Jews and other outcasts have died in the extermination camps, but Schindler has saved more than eleven hundred Jews by employing them in his company.

One of the closing scenes in the movie made me sob.

The year is 1945, and the Nazis have surrendered. Mr. Schindler and his wife are preparing to leave the company's headquarters. As he walks from his factory building to his car, he is surrounded by Jewish workers who owe him their lives. But as he approaches his car, he begins wondering why he kept it. It could have been sold to save ten more people. Then he notices a small gold pin attached to his coat lapel. Sobbing, he drops to his knees. He is sobbing because he suddenly realizes that his little pin, if he had sold it, could have purchased a life. During the war, one pin equaled one person in value—and he chose the pin.

Mr. Schindler is, at that very moment, taking account of how he has lived his life, and the realization that he has not done all he could have done leaves him devastated.

In Romans 14:12, Paul also says, "So then each of us

will give an account of himself to God." A day is coming when each of us will look our Lord in the eyes and explain our lives to Him. We will be answering the question: "What have you done with what I've entrusted to you?"

Wow! That's an intense question to be asked by the One who made and knows and sees everything!

What's your answer to that question at this point in your life? Examine yourself (see 2 Corinthians 13:5). How have you used the time, the money, the talents, and the resources He has given you? Look at your actions, your decisions, your attitudes, your conversations, your calendar, and your checkbook for hints about what you will hear coming from your own lips on that day.

Thankfully, every day we wake up brings new mercies and a new chance to live for His glory. Can you think of a better choice that you can make today? Make the decision to seek to live more for God's purposes than for your own. To live for other people's benefit rather than your own pleasure.

In his moment of reckoning before a thousand witnesses, Mr. Schindler didn't see the good he had done. He saw instead the good he had the power to do but didn't—and that truth brought him to his knees.

When we appear before the King at the end of our

lives, I have a feeling we will all be on our faces before Him. But I know I want to live my life so that my Lord will smile and nod and say to me, "Well done, good and faithful servant. Come. Dine with me" (see Matthew 25:21).

Question

What will your answer be on the day you are face-to-face with God? How will you live differently today so that the answer on that day might make the King of kings smile? Think of a few tangible examples of ways you can reach out to someone in your life because of what God has given you.

Lord, help me to live my life today so that on my last day I will be able to tell You about things that make You proud. I want to be intentional about living for You. Give me the strength to try every day to live with the awareness that You died for me, that You saved me. Give me the desire to be worthy of You, Lord. I know I will never do everything right, but please help me to live a life worthy of the faith You've called me to. Amen.

4.7

ACTION DAY #4

You cannot do a kindness too soon,
for you never know how soon it will be too late.

RALPH WALDO EMERSON

This is the final Action Day in your *My 30 Days Under the Overpass* experience (but hopefully not the last one of your life). I hope you've had some awesome encounters that have pulled you out of your comfort zone and closer to God.

By now I hope you've also noticed how easy it is to make a difference in someone's life. Your old clothes, your bag of groceries, your two hours—these small gifts can impact many lives and show others a real example of a person living out their faith in Jesus Christ. This is powerful stuff with eternal reverberations.

Of course, you need to decide whether you're going

to continue living this way once you finish this book.

Christianity is a lifestyle of faithful pursuit of Jesus Christ, not just a great week or two of spiritual adventure.

Here are three options for today. As you consider them, know that I've been praying for you.

OPTION 1: DINNER MENU

Go out to dinner with your family or with some friends tonight. Don't decide on the restaurant just yet. Spend some time walking around before you go in to dinner and find a restaurant that has a homeless man or woman sitting nearby. After you have your table, grab the menu and head out to the homeless person and offer to purchase them any meal they want off of the menu. Spend some time talking to them while they're deciding, answering their amazed question as to why you're doing what you're doing. Head back inside and order the homeless person's meal to-go, then take it outside as soon as it arrives.

OPTION 2: BARE ESSENTIALS

Ever been stranded somewhere without your toothbrush? How did you smell the day you forgot to put on deodorant?

For many of the men and women on the streets, the bare essentials of hygiene are not something that's easily acquired. Grab a few friends and head to the local grocery store. Buy some deodorant, a few toothbrushes and tubes of toothpaste, some soap, some travel shampoos, some instant hand sanitizer. Head downtown and walk around to find some homeless individuals to offer a few of the supplies to. Not everyone will want what you're offering. Maybe it's the wrong kind (homeless people have favorite kinds of stuff just like you and I do). Offer it without assuming that they will instantly accept. See what their response is! Save whatever you have left over for a later date, or head to a nearby shelter or food pantry and drop off the supplies there.

OPTION 3: YOUR OWN BIG IDEA

I'm sure by now you get the general idea of what an Action Day option is all about. What is the Lord putting on your heart? Maybe there's something you can do for a person you've met during the last thirty days? Maybe there's a "What if...?" question lurking in the back of your mind that needs to be explored a little further. Call up a few friends, maybe some who are going through this devotional with you, maybe some who aren't. Go to a coffee shop and talk about, pray about, and plan out an Action Day option of your own, and then go do it.

Now, put down the devotional and spend some serious time on your knees before the Lord, asking Him to direct your decisions, your steps, your every move and every word. Ask for the courage to step out in bold ways and *live* the gospel that you believe. Pray for the endurance to continue doing it even after the final pages of this devotional have been read. Go and let the King of kings love others through you.

> *Lord, thank You for all the chances that I've had to take the ideas in this devotional and apply them to real life and real people. You've covered my mistakes and shown me incredible things. Please do that again today as I go out into the world around me. Show me what You would have me do, and help me to reflect You in my conversations, my thoughts, and my actions. Amen.*

NOTES TO SELF

[REFLECTIONS ON WEEK FOUR]

a. Something God showed me this week:

b. A question I've pondered this week:

c. Someone I met this week I want to remember:

d. A decision I've made this week to change how I live:

e. More notes to self:

GUT CHECK 2.0

Remember when we first did the Gut Check? Here's your chance to reflect a little more deeply on what has gone on inside of you during these last thirty days. Spend some time thinking through and answering these questions. After you finish these questions, take a few quick moments to go back to Gut Check 1.0 and see how you've changed and grown.

1. How have I grown during these thirty days? What are some ways that I think about myself, others, and God differently?

2. What are some things that I still would like to see change about my faith, my comfort zone, and my willingness to step outside of what's normal in order to love people and meet needs?

3. What is a place (e.g., school, downtown, home) where I'm more willing to stand up for my faith? What is a place where it's still hard for me to live what I believe?

4. What will be hard about continuing to live with the things I've learned in this devotional?

5. Next year, what is one thing I want to remember about these past thirty days?

6. Now when I see a homeless person on the sidewalk when I'm downtown, what will I do?

7. What is a possession that would be really hard for me to part with? Am I any more willing to let it go now than I was before I started this devotional?

8. Write a few sentences about what it means to tangibly love God and love others.

OFF-RAMP

*Take care lest you forget
the LORD your God.*
DEUTERONOMY 8:11

Wow. It's been thirty days already. If your life is half as busy as I think it is, then these few days have really flown by. Thanks for journeying with me. It has been a real pleasure to share some of my own stories and experiences with you.

I trust that God has revealed a lot to you about who you are, who He is, and the world in which you live. There's no such thing as a "coincidence" in a universe created by an omnipotent God. Things happen for a reason. Your picking up this book was no accident, nor were the conversations, thoughts, experiences, and lessons you've had because of it.

The big question now is whether or not those experiences will stick with you after you close the final pages of this devotional.

Remembering is hard.

A few months after Sam and I returned to "normal life," I stopped to buy lunch, even though I was late for a meeting. I walked hurriedly into a burrito shop, stood impatiently in line, quickly ordered the burrito, paid, and walked out. As I sped down the freeway toward my meeting, I practically inhaled the burrito in less than ten minutes. As I slurped up the last bit of iced tea from the cup and crumpled the foil into a ball to toss aside, I was slammed with a vivid memory from the streets.

One afternoon Sam and I had panhandled for four hours in order to buy a single burrito to split between the two of us. The thankfulness I had felt that evening as we hungrily enjoyed the half-burrito cast my present lack of gratitude in an embarrassing light. Just a few months prior, I had been overjoyed by half a burrito after hours of sitting on the hot sidewalk begging for other people's money.

Why was I now acting as though all I had learned during an intense five-month experience on the streets really didn't matter?

As humans, we're enormously forgetful. The strange

thing about it is that most of us don't feel forgetful until something in the present reminds us of what happened in the past.

That is one of the challenges you will face as this daily book comes to a close. I hope that the things we've talked about, the Scripture passages we've looked at, the experiences of serving other people even when it's difficult and inconvenient, and all that we've done during these last thirty days have had a strong impact on you.

But more than that, I hope and pray that the effect of all you've gone through during the past weeks sticks with you and continues to influence the way you live your life every day. The homeless people you reached out to, the outcasts in your school you befriended, the coworkers you had conversations with will be there tomorrow, even after this devotional stops reminding you to notice them.

How can you help make the changes you've experienced stick?

Practice remembering.

The verse in Deuteronomy says, "Take care lest you forget the LORD your God." Take care. That means *doing* something intentional to help you remember what God has shown you. That's one of the reasons for the "Notes to Self" sections in this devotional. You've had a chance to jot down thoughts, questions, and people's names, save photographs, and record experiences.

Make a point a few weeks from now to sit down for an hour or so and look back through this book and let the memories from the past shock your present.

Practice remembering.

Maybe it looks like grabbing a few friends and going out for coffee and helping one another remember what you went through together during these thirty days. Sam and I do that every now and then when we talk. We remember Norm and David and Pamela. Sometimes the memories are hard, sometimes funny, sometimes embarrassing. But the process of remembering reconnects us to the landscapes the Lord has asked us to walk through.

Practice remembering.

Maybe it looks like committing to go down and visit the same people you've been able to connect with during the past thirty days for the next thirty days. Volunteer at the same mission, do another clothing drive, make more spaghetti dinners.

Remember: We aren't called to change the entire world. But we are called to love others in Christ's name and to help make a difference one person at a time, one need at a time.

We are called to live loud!

MORE INFO

Hungry for more information? The Internet is a great place to find out tons of stuff. Because a Google search for "homelessness" returns 17 *million* pages, here is a slightly shorter list of sites that I used to find the facts you read throughout the devotional:

1. www.agrm.org: The Association of Gospel Rescue Missions is a network of rescue missions across multiple countries. Most rescue missions have services for the homeless (food, clothing, shelter), as well as more in-depth rehabilitation facilities for those men and women working toward sobriety and a drug-free lifestyle.

2. www.nationalhomeless.org: The National Coalition for the Homeless is a national network of people who are currently experiencing or who have experienced

homelessness, activists and advocates, community-based and faith-based service providers, and others committed to ending homelessness.

3. www.hud.gov/homeless: The U.S. Department of Housing and Urban Development website is the place to find official U.S. government info regarding the homeless population in this country.

4. www.nmha.org: The National Mental Health Association is the country's oldest and largest nonprofit organization addressing all aspects of mental health and mental illness.

You can also find out more about me and my books at

www.undertheoverpass.com

THANKS

This book would simply not exist were it not for the awesome efforts and passion of many people. I'd like to express my thanks to several of these men and women of faith below.

Don Jacobson, publisher: Thank you for your vision and ideas about how *Under the Overpass* and this project can impact and encourage people! I admire the way you lead Multnomah, and I'm honored to know you.

David Kopp, editor: I could spend ten years pursuing doctoral work in English and not realize half the command of words you demonstrate. Thank you for the chance to work together again on this project!

Next Gen Team: I can't even begin to express all the gratitude I feel. Thanks for the countless phone calls, the coffee breaks, the fresh ideas, and the heart and passion to see this come together!

Multnomah Publishers: You are all tremendous. Thank you for the passion and effort you employ everyday to produce books that change people's lives. It's an honor to publish with you.

Debbie Diederich & 30 Hour Famine Team: Thank you for your love for our Lord and your heart for the youth of our world. I'm so excited to see how the Lord works through this to challenge and impact people for Him!

Danae: Where do I begin, Nae? I am yours, and forever better because of you. Seven months and a lifetime to come... I love you. Always.

You, the reader: Thank you for journeying with me these past 30 days. I hope that someday I can learn at least a little about what the Lord has done in you during these past thirty days. I'm stoked you're still reading! Live loud!